# Hear, Listen, Play!

# Hear, Listen, Play!

## HOW TO FREE YOUR STUDENTS' AURAL, IMPROVISATION, AND PERFORMANCE SKILLS

## **Lucy Green**

Institute of Education, University of London, UK

OXFORD
UNIVERSITY PRESS

# OXFORD
## UNIVERSITY PRESS

Oxford University Press is a department of the University of Oxford. It furthers the University's objective of excellence in research, scholarship, and education by publishing worldwide.

Oxford    New York

Auckland    Cape Town    Dar es Salaam    Hong Kong    Karachi
Kuala Lumpur    Madrid    Melbourne    Mexico City    Nairobi
New Delhi    Shanghai    Taipei    Toronto

With offices in

Argentina    Austria    Brazil    Chile    Czech Republic    France    Greece
Guatemala    Hungary    Italy    Japan    Poland    Portugal    Singapore
South Korea    Switzerland    Thailand    Turkey    Ukraine    Vietnam

Oxford is a registered trade mark of Oxford University Press in the UK and certain other countries.

Published in the United States of America by
Oxford University Press
198 Madison Avenue, New York, NY 10016

Library of Congress Cataloging-in-Publication Data
Green, Lucy.
Hear, listen, play! : how to free your student's aural, improvisation and performance skills / Lucy Green.
pages cm
ISBN 978-0-19-999576-9 (alk. paper)
1. Music—Instruction and study. 2. Improvisation (Music) I. Title.
MT1.G818 2013
780.71—dc23        2013014508

5   7   9   8   6

Printed in the United States of America on acid-free paper

In loving memory of my mother, Mary Portch Green
1925–2012

# CONTENTS

# ACKNOWLEDGEMENTS

This book has been more than fifteen years in the making. During that period innumerable organisations and individuals have shared their experience, expertise, support, and advice. The teams who made up the research projects, Musical Futures and the Ear Playing Project; the musicians who participated in the How Popular Musicians Learn project; and all the teachers and students who gave their time, took risks, shared their views, and allowed me to work closely with them are owed an incalculable debt. I am grateful to every one of them and sad that there are too many to include all their names here.

Amongst organisations, I would like to name the Paul Hamlyn Foundation, the Esmée Fairbairn Foundation, the Associated Board of the Royal Schools of Music, the Royal Institute for Blind People, and my own college, the London University Institute of Education. The work has also received support from numerous other music education organisations in the UK, to whom we remain extremely grateful.

Amongst individuals, I have been most fortunate to have had as my research assistants three wonderful people: Abigail D'Amore, David Baker, and Maria Varvarigou. Abigail was my assistant in the original Musical Futures informal learning project and is now the Project Leader for Musical Futures as a whole; she was also the external evaluator of the Ear Playing Project. She and I collected most of the classroom data together, and she, along with Dave Price and the Musical Futures team, has since disseminated the work through their visionary continuing professional development for teachers. David Baker and Maria Varvarigou were research officers in the Ear Playing Project. David took charge especially of the experiment reported in appendix A and the ensemble work; Maria was particularly involved in collecting and analysing data related to learning styles. In addition to these roles, all three made contributions throughout every aspect of all the work in a myriad of ways. Without their constant vigilance, wisdom, and commitment this book would not have been written.

Colleagues and teachers who have given detailed and insightful comments on a draft of the present text include June Bonfield-Brown, Sue Pluthero, Ros Wheeler, and Ann Wright; the text has also benefited from encouragement, responses, testing, and help of various kinds from Kim Bloomfield, Anna Gower, Isobel Marshall, Thuy Huang, and Sophie Ford.

Amongst many others who participated in the projects and made invaluable contributions are John Witchell, Nigel Scaife, James Risdon, Sally Zimmerman, Maria Vraka, John Holmes, and Chris Harrison.

My husband, Charlie Ford, gave all the support any writer could want from their partner, including reading the text in detail and being prepared to discuss endless issues arising from the work, over many years.

I would like to thank Musical Futures and Emile Holba for the classroom photos, and David Baker for the photos of work in the instrumental and ensemble settings. I am delighted to have such lovely photos in the book, and would also like to thank the various schools, and the students and teachers depicted for their permission and cooperation.

Thanks to the students from the Guildhall School of Music, the Broken Record Project, Gareth Dylan Smith, Tim Smart, Marcus Ford, and Evangelos Himonides for their various roles in making the audio tracks.

Norm Hirschy, Erica Woods Tucker, and the team at Oxford University Press have been meticulous and unfailingly patient; and there is a special thank you for Rebecca Winfield.

★

Parts of the introductory sections titled "Why informal learning?" "Why popular music?" and "How do popular musicians learn?" are excerpted and edited by kind permission of the publishers from Lucy Green, *Music, Informal Learning and the School: A New Classroom Pedagogy* (Farnham: Ashgate, 2008), 5–10. Copyright © 2008.

# NOTE ON THE TEXT

This handbook is based on and incorporates findings from extensive and systematic research over many years. Nonetheless, it is not an academic text. Any readers interested in following up the more technical sides of the research, or looking in more detail at the findings and how they relate to other scholarly work, are directed to the appendices. Appendix A gives information about an experiment which discovered that a sample of students aged ten to fourteen who used the methods gained higher scores in a formal aural test than their counterparts who did not use the methods. I have included these results since such statistics can be helpful if advocating new approaches to parents, head teachers, and other interested parties. Other than that, the text is non-academic. However, for the curious reader appendix B contains a list of the academic texts on which the handbook is directly based; appendix C contains a list of related research and discussions by other writers; and appendix D gives a list of websites with further information and illustrations.

I hope that putting together into one binding, a teaching strategy addressed to a range of teaching contexts will be of use. Although many teachers regard themselves as specialists, that is, specialist instrumental teachers, band directors, or classroom teachers who work with particular age groups, nowadays more and more music teachers are spreading their activities across a range of contexts. Some may be interested in more than one part of the book for that reason. Although different music education settings have their own specificities, at a fundamental level, all forms of music education must share a degree of commonality. Even teachers who work predominantly in one setting can benefit from an understanding and application of teaching strategies in others, and from viewing the musical needs and capabilities of students in a holistic light. Thus, the teacher who works solely in the instrumental studio or in the teenage classroom, for example, may be interested in finding out how the strategies described here can work in environments different from their normal habitat. Furthermore, at a practical level, some of the strategies can quite easily be transported from the setting in which they are embedded in this book to another setting. An instrumental teacher could put four students together and carry out the free-choice exercise as described for the classroom; an ensemble leader could split up the ensemble into small groups for a few lessons and do likewise; a classroom teacher working with the whole class could do the exercise that is described here for ensembles, and so on.

The handbook can be used with one-to-one instrumental students at all levels; ensembles, including bands, orchestras, and other instrumental groups of any kind; and classroom students aged from around ten to eighteen or beyond, in both elective and generalist settings. Some of the strategies can be used in teacher-training sessions where teachers are being introduced to informal or aural ways of working, as well as with pre-service or trainee teachers and music undergraduates. The methods were designed for instruments rather than voices, and in the one-to-one setting, for pitched rather than unpitched instruments. However, the methods have also been tried with success using voices only; they lend themselves in the classroom and band environments to any instruments including unpitched percussion; and in the classroom setting in particular, students often choose to include singing as a central part of their activities.

The approach involves holistic learning rather than a graded system: learners tackle the task at their own level and in their own individual ways. The activities encourage learner autonomy, choice, and enjoyment in playing by ear; and they can increase confidence, heighten listening skills, and expand musical horizons. They also feed directly into the skills needed for improvisation and creativity. It is important to stress that the strategies are not designed in any way to replace existing approaches that teachers already use. Rather, they are intended to run alongside or in-between whatever other work teachers are already doing.

Quotations from teachers and students, and transcripts of teaching-and-learning encounters are all drawn from research, which took place in real contexts. Some of them have been slightly edited for purposes of clarification and illustration. However much of the idiomatic and sometimes ungrammatical speech of children and teenagers is largely untouched. The purpose of the citations is to give readers the opportunity to be a "fly-on-the-wall" during lessons, and to hear the voices of participants who have tried the teaching-and-learning strategies themselves. All names are pseudonyms.

The research for this handbook was carried out in England, but it has been written with the intention that it should be accessible for international usage. Classroom teachers and others in Wales, Scotland, and Northern Ireland, and in parts of Australia, Canada, the United States, Singapore, Uganda, Brazil, Bali, and Thailand, amongst other places, have used the strategies with success. So long as adequate space and equipment is available, the results are likely to be much as the same as those reported here. There is also no reason to suppose that classically trained instrumental teachers in different parts of the world would have different results. The strategies are based on a real-life method of music learning, which in its most fundamental sense is as old as music itself. In this sense it transcends local contexts of time and place and is, I believe, capable of being flexibly adapted to a range of contexts, according to the professional judgement and experience of the teacher. Teachers in some countries have been accustomed to working in broadly similar ways to those described here for many years, although of course every approach has its differences.

Owing to the intended international applicability of the strategies, I have avoided references to particular national curricula, national standards, governmental edicts, syllabi, or other factors likely to be specific to any one country or region, and which are in any case liable to change. The only exception to this is the occasional reference to grades, which occurs in the speech of participants from time to time.

A "grade" in this context refers to a system of instrumental exams from Preparatory through Grade 1 (beginner) to Grade 8 (advanced) and beyond to Diploma standard. To give an idea of the standards, Grade 1 would be taken on average after a year or so of lessons; Grade 6 would normally be required for entry to a general music degree in a UK university; and Grade 8 (usually with Distinction), would be the minimum for entry to a performance degree in a conservatoire. The largest exam boards, such as the Associated

Board of the Royal Schools of Music (ABRSM) and Trinity College have a major international reach, with exams being taken by hundreds of thousands of students in countries throughout the world. There are also similar systems for rock grades, the largest of which is Rock School. Any student of any age from early childhood to adulthood can take any grade, as and when they and/or their teacher feel the time is right.

# NOTE ON THE COMPANION WEBSITE

The teaching-and-learning strategies are linked to audio tracks which are freely available for download on www.oup.com/us/hearlistenplay. You may access the audio resources with username Music5 and password Book1745. Please note that these are case sensitive.

The materials consist of eight pieces of music, each of which is presented in full, then in parts. The first one is presented for C instruments and also for B-flat instruments; the others are in their original keys only. The pieces are:

- "Dreaming," a specially composed popular style piece produced electronically.

- "Link Up," a specially composed popular style piece played by a live band.

- Mozart's *Eine Kleine Nachtmusik*, opening, played by a string quartet.

- Beethoven's "Für Elise," first section, played on the piano.

- Clara Schumann's Piano Trio, op. 17, opening of the slow movement, played by violin, cello, and piano.

- Handel's Flute Sonata, op. 1, no. 5, Minuet, played by flute with harpsichord and cello continuo.

- Brahms's Symphony no. 1, 4th movement theme, arranged for string quartet with some help from an electronic keyboard.

- Bach's "Minuet in G," from the Anna Magdalena book, played on the harpsichord.

Further guidance about how the tracks are used as part of the teaching-and-learning strategies is given at appropriate points in the text. A full track listing and credits are available in appendices E and F, as well as on the website.

# INTRODUCTION

This handbook is primarily for classically trained instrumental and classroom music teachers, band directors, and those who lead orchestras and other kinds of ensembles. Its main focus is on the practicalities of putting into action a set of teaching-and-learning strategies derived from the informal learning practices of popular musicians. Why are these learning practices worthy of attention for music educators; what do they involve; and how do they differ from formal music education? The learning practices of popular musicians are simple, effective, flexible, and enjoyable. Shared in different ways by folk, jazz, and many other musicians, they can lead to high levels of skill-development, particularly in the realms of ear-playing and improvisation. Furthermore, many of the skills involved can be just as relevant to classical music as to any other musical style.

It can be helpful to conceive of informal popular music learning practices as having five main characteristics, and to identify some of the fundamental ways in which these differ from formal music education. These are of course not necessarily the only five characteristics, or the only way to conceive of them, but together, they represent merely one "thumbnail definition."

1. Informal learning in the popular sphere starts with music that the learners choose for themselves—music that is therefore familiar, well liked, and enjoyed. Very often the learners have a strong affinity and identity with the music. This is somewhat different from what normally happens in formal education, where teachers or other experts choose most of the music for the learners, and where the music is often likely to be unfamiliar to them.

2. One of the main methods of instrumental and vocal skill-acquisition involves copying recordings by ear, initially on a trial-and-error basis. On one hand, this requires conscious, highly attentive listening, linked to close copying. On the other hand, the learners also develop a more unconscious aural awareness of a wide range of music in and beyond the relevant style. These approaches have far-reaching differences from those based primarily on notation or other written or verbal instructions.

3. Informal learning takes place alone and also very importantly alongside friends, who share skills and knowledge through peer-group learning. Rather than being taught by an expert or adult with greater skill, the young learners help each other; they also learn more unconsciously simply by listening to and watching each other, and by talking about music. This occurs almost entirely in the absence of adult supervision or guidance, as distinct from the formal educational realm where there is usually a teacher or other more experienced person to lead the activities.

4. Skills and knowledge tend to be assimilated in holistic, haphazard ways, starting with whole, real-world pieces of music; and each learner finds their own

route through the learning. In the formal realm, by contrast, learners tend to follow a structured route based on teachers' or other experts' understanding of progression from simple to complex. This often involves specially composed music, a curriculum or a graded syllabus.

5. Finally, informal approaches tend to involve a particularly deep integration of listening, performing, improvising, and composing throughout the learning process. This is rather different from what happens in formal music education, where we are liable to split skills up into different lessons or sections of lessons.

## How could informal learning practices relate to formal music education?

The Hear-Listen-Play approach—or HeLP approach—in this handbook is based on a distillation and adaption of popular musicians' learning practices. The overall aims are:

- To give music students of all ages and abilities a relevant, accessible, and enjoyable skill, which research suggests many of them may not otherwise come across, and which they can continue to build on for the rest of their lives if they wish.

- To give music teachers—especially those who are classically trained and may feel unfamiliar with the realms of ear-playing or informal learning—some simple strategies, which research suggests they are likely to find helpful and interesting in a range of ways.

The HeLP approach helps teachers to help students to move from hearing, towards listening to music, then playing what they are listening to. In so doing, it frees their aural, improvisation, and performance skills.

## The organisation and use of the handbook

The handbook is organised in three parts, each of which is geared towards a different teaching-and-learning context, although some teachers are likely to work across more than one of these contexts. I refer to the three contexts as "instrumental tuition," "ensembles" and "classrooms" respectively. In the classroom context, the students are divided into small friendship groups. This is why I use the word "ensembles" to distinguish teacher-directed instructional and rehearsal groups from "small groups" formed within classrooms.

- Part 1 is for instrumental tuition at any level. By "instrumental tuition" I mean the kind of teaching that normally takes place on a one-to-one basis. It is specialist, and the teacher will be an expert player on the instrument or instruments being taught. Some instrumental teachers work entirely in their own home or studio; others may work in schools, where students are timetabled to see them individually or in small groups. Where groups of more than two or three students are being taught at a time, part 2 would be more relevant.

- Part 2 is for ensembles, meaning small groups of students learning to play specialist orchestral or band instruments; larger mixed groups such as orchestras, marching bands, jazz bands, and others in schools and community music settings; small groups such as string quartets; and also any kind of other ad hoc group—for example, one of our research groups included a number of ukuleles, a euphonium, some violins, guitars, keyboards, unpitched percussion, and other instruments. Some ensembles meet in schools as part of the school timetable; others meet for extracurricular activities; others may be part of a community programme. For rock bands or other similar groups, however, part 3 would be more relevant.

- Part 3 is for classrooms. This refers to a range of contexts found in schools, involving children from around age ten upwards, and young people up to any age. In some contexts these will be generalist classrooms where music is an entitlement subject for everyone and where the group has a wide mix of ability and prior musical experience. In others, the classroom may be a specialist one where students have elected for the subject and where they all have a certain level of ability and experience. Some classroom-type work can go on as an extracurricular, voluntary activity, and in some cases this might include the encouragement of rock bands. In all such settings, the strategies require that the students are divided into small friendship groups playing a mix of any kind of instruments.

Each section of the book is written for each of these specific settings. Within each setting there are recommended stages of the teaching-and-learning strategies, involving three stages in the instrumental and classroom realms, and only one in the ensemble context. However, some teachers may prefer to reorder the stages, to choose only one or two of them, or to repeat them at different times. Although the audio materials are the same in each setting, not all the materials are used in all the settings; and the materials are used in a different order and a different way within each setting.

Each section begins with a description of who has participated in the research phase of the strategies. This is followed by the basic recommended steps involved in putting the strategies into practice. Then there is a description of what you are likely to witness in the behaviour and responses of the students, if you choose to try out the strategies. Following this is a section discussing the role of the teacher in more detail. This is illustrated with examples of teaching strategies, presented as transcripts of what really happened in encounters between a teacher and one or more students, during the research. Finally, each section ends with some examples of what participants have said about their experiences of using the strategies, which I hope will bring to life some of the discussions.

Some readers may prefer to skip parts of the text, and it was written with that in mind. For example, it is not necessary to read the whole section about how popular musicians learn, or to peruse every transcribed quote from every student or teacher, in order to be able to use the strategies oneself. For practical purposes, the most important sections within each part are the "Preliminary practicalities," the "Basic steps," and the "Teaching strategies." However, as mentioned in the Note on the Text, teachers may benefit from reading in areas beyond their normal work context. Many of those who participated in the research kindly read a draft of the book. Several commented they were glad they had read the whole text, otherwise they would have missed interesting things they would not have expected to be relevant to them, but which turned out to be so.

The strategies were developed especially for classically trained teachers, to whom this way of learning music is likely to be unfamiliar; although in the research, teachers with experience of informal learning in a range of jazz, popular, folk, and traditional music also found them helpful. Some teachers may wish to try the strategies with all their students, while others may wish to select a few individuals, ensembles, or classes they feel might particularly benefit. The strategies can be carried out in only a few lessons or rehearsals, and in the case of the instrumental work, in just part of each lesson; and they need not in any way affect other lessons or other aspects of teachers' work. However, the majority of the teachers involved have reported a beneficial effect on their teaching in general.

## The audio materials: an overview

The audio materials are provided on the website www.oup.com/us/hearlistenplay (username: Music5; password: Book1745). Purchase of this handbook carries with it permission to make as many copies of the tracks as are needed.

Below is a description of the materials. It might make them sound rather complicated but they are actually very straightforward: a quick glance at the track lists in appendix E, or a quick listen to a few bars on the website, should make it all clear.

The materials are grouped into two sections: "Popular-style pieces," and "Classical pieces." The pieces are used in a different way and a different order within the three teaching contexts addressed in the handbook.

For each piece, the full arrangement is presented on the first track. Then the subsequent tracks each present a separate part, played on its own, and repeated over and over for approximately two minutes. Apart from the first piece, the repeated tracks are not electronically looped but played live, to avoid sounding mechanical. In the case of the two popular style pieces, there is first the bass riff, then a selection of the other parts, increasing in difficulty. In the case of the classical pieces, there is first a simplified version in two parts, then the melody, then the bass part separately. Where the melody or bass is over a certain length, it is presented in two sections, each on its own track.

The first piece and all its tracks are given twice, once for C instruments, and once for B-flat instruments. The other pieces are all played live, and are given in their original keys; however both B-flat and E-flat instruments have used them successfully. The popular style pieces were especially composed in order to avoid complicated recording, performing, and composition copyright issues. They are:

- "Dreaming": this is based on an eight-bar repeated phrase, with a bass line, a piano part with bass and triadic harmony, a few other elements, and a "codetta." It was prepared using electronic samples.

- "Link Up": this contains a number of riffs, most of which are four bars long, with one of two bars. It is performed by a live band, but has also been used during the research in a very simple electronic keyboard version.

Within the classical group are six pieces, all in their original keys. Again, they have been tried by a range of instruments including C, B-flat, and E-flat instruments. They are:

- Mozart's *Eine Kleine Nachtmusik*, opening, played by a string quartet.

- Beethoven's "Für Elise," first section, played on the piano.

- Clara Schumann's Piano Trio, op. 17, the opening of the slow movement, played by violin, cello, and piano.

- Handel's Flute Sonata, op. 1, no. 5, Minuet played by flute with harpsichord and cello continuo.

- Brahms's Symphony no. 1, 4th movement theme, arranged for string quartet with some help from an electronic keyboard.

- Bach's "Minuet in G," from the Anna Magdalena book, played on a harpsichord.

The given materials are available to demonstrate the suggested strategies and to get you started, but they are of course only a small sample of musical styles, focussing on the popular and the classical spheres. Some teachers may wish to make their own materials, in a range of styles, and this is to be encouraged. If you are unfamiliar with ear-playing I would recommend that the strategies are tried out first using the given materials with a few students before developing your own materials, as it will be helpful to witness how they work.

## Why informal learning?

By the term "formal" music education I refer partly to types of institution and partly to types of practice. Formal music education usually contains one or more of the following: educational institutions from primary schools to conservatoires, partly involving or entirely dedicated to the teaching and learning of music; instrumental and vocal teaching programmes running either within or alongside these institutions; written curricula, syllabi, or explicit teaching traditions; professional teachers, lecturers, or master musicians who in most cases possess some form of relevant qualifications; systematic assessment mechanisms such as grade exams, national school exams, or university exams; a variety of qualifications such as diplomas and degrees; music notation, which is sometimes regarded as peripheral but more usually is central; and finally, a body of literature, including texts on music, pedagogical texts, and teaching materials. Historically, formal music education of this kind has been associated primarily with the transmission of Western classical music, although increasingly it is bringing an ever-widening range of musical styles within its purview.

Alongside or instead of formal music education there are in every society other ways of passing on and acquiring musical skills and knowledge, usually associated with various types of what can be called "vernacular" music. These are what I refer to as informal learning practices. At the extreme end, no syllabus, curriculum, exams, or teacher are involved. Primarily, these learning practices rely on the participants' enculturation or immersion in the music and musical practices of their environment. Whereas some level of familiarity with the music being learnt is a fundamental factor needed in all aspects of music learning, enculturation plays a particularly prominent part in informal learning. In the traditional music of many countries, for example, young children are drawn into group music-making activities on a daily basis, both within the home and beyond, almost from birth. Through being included in music making by adults and older children around them, they pick up musical skills in ways that are similar to how they acquire linguistic skills. Most folk and traditional musics are learnt informally in such ways, by extended immersion in listening to, watching, and imitating the music and music-making practices of the surrounding community. Within various types of popular music too, young musicians often teach themselves or pick up skills and knowledge, often with the help or encouragement of their family or peers, by watching and imitating musicians around them, and by listening to recordings or performances and other live events involving their chosen music. They bring to these activities high levels of motivation and enjoyment, and in some cases they go on to become extremely proficient musicians.

The distinction between formal music education and informal music learning, however, is rarely absolutely clear-cut. In many cases the two areas merge, and each may combine elements of the other. In some vernacular music, as well as in many art musics of the world such as Indian classical music and to a large extent jazz, there are systems of what might be called "apprenticeship training" whereby young musicians are either trained or guided by an adult community of expertise: a sitar guru in India, the Akan master drummer, the samba schools of Rio de Janeiro, the Irish session, or the group-learning methods of Javanese Gamelan are just a few examples. The Internet has rapidly developed into one of the most accessible media for learning to play a vast range of different instruments in different styles. This involves a mix of a "virtual teacher" who instructs, and an informal setting where the learner can switch off the teacher at any time, and there is no retribution for not doing the assigned tasks between sessions!

Some musicians have one foot in the formal sphere, and the other foot in the informal sphere; and many musicians who are brought up mainly in one, also experience the other to some extent. For example, increasing numbers of classically trained musicians, especially amongst the younger generation, also play jazz or popular music, where they learn their skills mainly informally. Many learners who would have been solidly located in the informal realm a few decades ago, are taking advantage of formal studies such as lessons on a range of instruments for which it would have been difficult until recently to find a professional, qualified teacher. Some musicians take national qualifications, from elementary exams to postgraduate degrees, which are now available in various forms of vernacular music. There is also fast-growing provision through community music networks and many other organisations, which sit somewhere between the formal and the informal spheres.

In spite of these overlaps between the formal and the informal, there are some fundamental features of informal learning, which are shared in different ways by many popular, folk, traditional, jazz, and other musicians, and which are distinct from the main approaches associated with Western classical music. These learning practices are, at root, aural.

## Why popular music?

Although informal learning practices can be shared across many styles of music, there are likely to be some crucial differences specifically relating to the transmission processes of popular music, broadly defined. These differences are tempting to overlook but are potentially very significant for music education. First, unlike in most folk and traditional fields, most young popular musicians are not regularly surrounded by an adult community of practising popular musicians whom they can talk to, listen to, watch, and imitate, or who initiate them into relevant skills and knowledge. Young popular musicians tend to engage in a significant amount of solitary learning, primarily using recordings as their main resource. Second, in so far as a community of practice is available to these young musicians, it tends to be a community of peers rather than master musicians or adults with greater skills.

The significance of these two factors is quite profound, as they affect the entire way in which skills and knowledge are transmitted in the popular music field. They take the onus of transmission away from an authority figure, expert, or older member of the family or community and put it largely into the hands of the young learners themselves. In this sense, young learners in popular music embark upon a journey which is different not only from the learning associated with Western classical music but in many ways from folk and traditional approaches too..

The specific ways in which popular musicians go about acquiring their skills and knowledge vary between different substyles of popular music, different national, social, and cultural contexts, and from one individual learner to another, the more so precisely because of the general lack of formal systematisation involved in such learning. In spite of such differences, though, informal popular-music learning practices are undertaken in one way or another by most popular musicians in nearly all substyles, in ways that can be characterised by a number of general features. The practices that form the backbone to the strategies in this handbook are based primarily on a study of popular musicians who play instruments (including the voice) and participate in bands, rather than those who are involved in DJ-ing, mixing, or producing music electronically.

## How do popular musicians learn?

Popular musicians tend to acquire musical skills and knowledge, first and foremost, through enculturation, that is, involvement with the music they are familiar with, which they like, and which they hear around and about them. Early on they start to experiment with an instrument or the voice, discovering what different sounds they can make through trial and error before stringing sounds together into embryonic musical phrases, rhythms, or harmonies.

The overriding learning practice for most popular musicians is to copy recordings by ear. This is not the same activity as the age-old practice of learning by listening to and aurally copying other musicians: it involves a recording rather than another human being. This difference has profound consequences. It also seems to me an extraordinary fact that the practice has developed in only the hundred years or so that have elapsed since the advent of recording technologies. Furthermore, it has developed across many countries of the world through the activities of children and young people, basically in isolation from each other, outside of any networking or formal structures, and largely without adult guidance.

It can be helpful to distinguish two approaches to this listening practice, each situated at the opposite ends of a pole. At one extreme there is what I call "purposive listening," that is, listening with the conscious purpose of adopting and adapting what is heard into one's own practices. At the other extreme there is "distracted listening." This occurs when music is heard in the background, and is not attended to in a focused way: it enters the mind almost entirely through unconscious enculturation. Both of these listening practices extend beyond the early learning stages and into professional realms, as popular musicians need to keep up with ever-changing trends.

Copying recordings is almost always a solitary activity, but solitude is not a distinguishing mark of the popular-music learner. On the contrary, group activities occurring in the absence of adult supervision or guidance are of great importance. They are characterised by two aspects. One is "peer-directed learning." This involves the conscious sharing of knowledge and skills or explicit peer teaching through, for example, demonstration of a rhythm or chord by one group member for the benefit of another. The other is "group learning," where there is no conscious demonstration or teaching as such, but where learning takes place through watching and imitation during music-making, as well as talking about music during and outside rehearsals.

Bands are formed at very early stages, even if the players have little control over their instruments and virtually no knowledge of any chord progressions, licks, or songs. Often they start up a band or a series of bands within a few months of beginning to play their instruments, mostly in their mid- to later teenage years. Schools are a vital social institution to band formation, even though most bands start up without the aid of teachers. Any instruments or practice spaces that the school can provide and, more importantly, the schools built-in population of hundreds of students, are crucial. Although early bands are nearly always formed with peers, age is less important than musical ability, and band members are all likely to be at a roughly similar standard.

Most bands involve themselves in a range of practices including jamming and other forms of improvisation, playing songs they know and like, and making up their own music. Conscious and unconscious peer-directed learning and group-learning take place: different band members will demonstrate learnt or original musical ideas to one another, and players will engage in joint compositions, which often involve all members of the band putting in their own ideas. All of this generally occurs in the absence of an adult or other person who can provide leadership or who has greater musical experience.

It is well known that notation plays little part in the popular music world, although it is used in a few cases such as highly professional function or theatre bands, or in an occasional manner such as when a musician scribbles something down on a piece of paper, usually to be thrown away as soon as the instruction is internalised. Session musicians are more likely to have constant work if they can read. But the main means of learning and passing on music is through recordings, either commercial ones or demos passed between the musicians. Even when notation is used, it is never used on its own but is always heavily mixed in with purposive listening and copying. I know of no statistical research on this currently, but it is reasonable to suppose that less than 40 percent of pop musicians know how to read staff notation, mostly having been introduced to it through some amount of formal music education. However, even given this guidance, when operating in the informal realm, such musicians nonetheless tend to adapt any notational skills to their own use in highly idiosyncratic ways.

Aural copying pays attention to a number of factors, which are not readily communicated through notation. These include idiosyncratic and nonstandardised timbres, rhythmic flexibility, pitch inflection, and many other aspects, not least those never-to-be-defined but always recognisable qualities such as "groove," "feel," and "swing." Here again, there is not only conscious, purposive listening and copying but also loose imitation related to continuous, unconscious enculturation and distracted listening. These are not only essential parts of the early learning process, but continue to be the principle means through which music is transmitted and reproduced throughout a popular musician's career.

The concept of technique as a conscious aspect of controlling the instrument or voice comes late to most popular musicians and in many cases is incorporated into their activities either immediately before, or some time after becoming professional. Thus, having taught themselves to play or sing in their own ways, the musicians adopt standard techniques at a late stage and this often comes with surprising ease.

As distinct from the executive psychomotor technique involved in playing or singing, popular musicians also acquire, to varying degrees, knowledge and understanding of musical technicalities or theory. Such comprehension usually comes haphazardly, according to whatever music is being played and enjoyed at the time. To begin with, the musicians are able to use musical elements in stylistically appropriate ways, but usually without being able to apply names to them or to discuss them in any but vague or metaphorical terms. Since listening is the prime source of learning, working out the relationships between sounds follows on from that. Thus learning about music theory tends to be led by excitement about the music. As time goes by the pieces of the musical jigsaw puzzle begin to fall into place, to differing degrees depending on the individual, which can often lead to highly sophisticated levels of theoretical knowledge and understanding. Not surprisingly, all this emphasis on listening also results in the development of perceptive and effective aural capacities.

Some musicians practise their instruments for five or six hours a day in the early stages of learning, others practise for considerably less time, and some hardly ever practise at all. Many tend to approach practice according to mood, other commitments in life, or motivation by external factors such as joining a new band or composing a new song. Their musical development is often marked by some periods of relatively intensive practice interspersed with other periods without any practice at all. Most importantly, practice is something they do only so long as they enjoy it.

Along with these learning practices go attitudes towards musical value and musical ability, which tend to emphasise expressive qualities such as "feel," "sensitivity," "spirit," or other similar attributes, over and above complexity or technical ability. Popular musicians also place high value on friendship amongst themselves, along with tolerance, shared taste, and commitment. I am not suggesting that all young popular musicians are exceptionally well-balanced individuals who never have arguments, but that cooperation, sensitivity to others, commitment, and responsibility are explicitly highly valued by the musicians. Furthermore, this emphasis on friendship and commitment concerns not only the social relationships that surround the band practice or performance but are necessary conditions of two additional aspects.

One is that, since the music being played is arrived at through choice and group negotiation, all the productive activities of the band are reliant on a consensus of taste and/or a willingness to tolerate the potentially differing tastes of others, as well as the ability to cooperate, and the responsibility of arriving at rehearsals and gigs at the correct place and time with the correct equipment. Without such cooperation (especially in the absence of incentives such as fame and money, but even *with* such incentives), a band will eventually disintegrate. A second aspect is that friendship, cooperation, and sensitivity to other people also affect the precise nature and feel of the music being produced, in ways that relate to musical communication in performance, and particularly to group composition and improvisation.

Playing popular music tends to raise the self-esteem and the perceived peer-group status of the participants. The values surrounding their music are intimately tied up with deeply felt issues of personal identity. Finally, in the informal realm there is no imperative to practise unless a learner feels like practising, no teacher or parent telling them they must do it, no homework, no coursework, no exams. One important thing that all popular musicians unfailingly report is the extremely high levels of enjoyment that accompany their music making and music-learning activities. From such a starting point, many go on to develop a deep passion for music, a thirst for listening to a wide range of styles, and a joyfulness in playing. It was in the hope of capturing some of that passion, thirst, and joy, and transferring these to a wider range of music learners that I initially started the research in this handbook.

# PART 1

# HeLP in instrumental settings

# Introduction

## The aims of HeLP in instrumental settings are:

- To show instrumental students some basic steps involved in ear-playing, which they may not otherwise come across, based on popular musicians' informal learning practices.

- To enhance students' enjoyment of music making and learning by opening out a likely new learning practice to them.

- To increase students' critical listening and appreciation skills.

- To increase students' pitch sense and rhythmic sense.

- To foster the beginnings of creative and improvisational abilities.

- To connect aural skills to a range of music, including drawing on students' existing tastes and knowledge.

- To support preparation for aural and practical musicianship tests in formal exams, at any level, and in any style of music.

- To give simple strategies to music teachers, particularly those who may not be familiar with ear-playing or informal learning.

- To enhance the confidence of teachers in ear-playing techniques.

- To give teachers insights into aspects of their students' musicality, of which they may have previously been unaware.

## Who participated in the instrumental research, and on which instruments?

The instrumental strategies have been tested in a research project called the Ear Playing Project http://earplaying.ioe.ac.uk, which was funded by the Esmée Fairbairn Foundation and supported by the London University Institute of Education. The project took place as a pilot study during the academic year 2008–9 and as a main study during 2011–12. Both studies involved putting aural-learning strategies into action for around seven to ten sessions of, on average fifteen minutes each.

The participants were:

- more than 54 teachers and 340 students, mostly in one-to-one settings.

4

We collected data through:

- 228 lesson observations involving 110 of the students and 21 of the teachers.

- 43 student interviews and 17 teacher interviews.

- 193 student questionnaires and 54 teacher questionnaires.

- E-mails, meetings and blog comments.

Most of the teachers were classically trained, but some had backgrounds in popular music, jazz, traditional music and music theatre. The piano was the most popular instrument, with around 66 percent of participants, but we also had students playing the recorder, flute, clarinet, oboe, bassoon, saxophone, euphonium, trumpet, trombone, violin, cello, and double bass. The students were between five and sixty-three years of age, with an average age of fourteen. Most of them had been playing for two or three years, but there were some beginners and some advanced learners.

# 2

# HeLP in instrumental settings: preliminary practicalities

## Audio materials

For an explanation of what is contained in the audio materials please see section 1: "The audio-materials: an overview" (xx) and appendix E, which contains a complete track listing. This is also shown on the handbook's accompanying website. For HeLP in the instrumental setting, both the popular style pieces and the classical pieces are recommended, starting with the popular ones first.

Once familiar with the strategies and the nature of the audio materials, teachers may wish to create their own specially tailored materials. You can also slow down the given tracks, or change their keys using a range of freely available software, if you wish to do so. The main characteristic of the materials, which is important to replicate, is that each part should involve a riff of two to four bars, which should be played continuously for about two minutes. This gives the students enough time to hear what is going on, try out notes, use notes as anchors, and keep on trying. It is probably best to try out the given materials yourself first so as to fully understand how they function.

## The time frame

The strategies can be put into practice for a mere ten to fifteen minutes as a portion of a normal weekly or fortnightly instrumental lesson, and most teachers found this an adequate amount of time. A few teachers felt that it was not long enough for the students to retain a good memory of the notes learnt, and some found it difficult to fit in the work and keep up all the other activities that they needed to cover each week. However, it is important to clarify that memorisation is not the point of the exercise; it is instead to give the student an opportunity to play from a recording by ear, with encouragement and guidance. Even if some students return the following week having done little or no practice during the week, and having largely forgotten the notes they learnt aurally the preceding week, you are likely to find that by repeating the exercise for just a short time each week, their ear-playing skills will improve. It is the ear-playing skills that are the main aim of the exercise, plus the fact that the student is discovering a new way to learn.

The activities, as described in part of the book, are organised in three stages:

• Stage 1: popular styles. In most cases it is best to start with one or more of the popular-style pieces in stage 1. If only one popular-style piece is chosen, this stage should take around three or four sessions; however some teachers and students may wish to use both popular-style pieces before tackling stage 2 and/ or to return to one of them later.

- Stage 2: classical music. Again, if only one classical piece is chosen, this stage should take about three sessions, but some teachers and students may wish to extend it by using more than one piece. Some will prefer to leave this stage out and go straight to stage 3; others may wish to revisit this stage later.

- Stage 3: Free choice. This should take about three or four sessions. Beyond that, depending on the individual student and teacher, you may wish to build on it, and this can of course continue for a life-time!

Different teachers may wish to modify the ordering and/or length of stages according to their own and their students' needs and interests. In order to clarify the stages and to illustrate their flexibility, please see section 4 for flowcharts of different possible combinations.

After completion of one or all the stages, teachers and students may wish to continue using the strategies with a range of other music, return to the materials and select different pieces, or introduce new stages such as improvisation or composition.

## Which instruments can be used?

The materials are appropriate for any chromatic pitched instrument tuned to equal temperament at A=440.

For pianists, if the instrument they are using is not at concert pitch, there are simple methods of digitally changing the pitch of the recording, without changing its speed, available on the Internet. (This is easier than retuning the piano!) I have not listed any websites or software here, as new ones develop rapidly, and old ones become obsolete. Alternatively, if the student has access to an electronic keyboard, one solution is for them to learn the music on that and then transfer it to the piano.

## Equipment needed for the lessons

As well as the instrument(s) being played, teachers will need a means of playing audio tracks in the teaching room. This could a CD player, a set of iPod speakers, a computer, or any other means.

## Home practice

It is not absolutely essential that all students practice at home, although naturally, those who do will improve faster, as with any other skill. However, we found differences amongst students' preferences in this regard.

On the one hand, some students prefer to do the ear-playing only during lessons, and in such cases it is important that they do not feel pressured to try it out at home:

It was harder at home because I didn't have someone to help me if I got totally stuck. (Piano student, twelve years old)

I enjoyed it in the lesson, but not much at home though. At school, there is always someone there, so, telling you if you are wrong or right and, then, you finally work it out. But, at home, I don't really have anyone with me. I have to work it out on my own, and I don't know if it is wrong or right. (Flute student, ten years old)

Well, when we had to practise it at home, there was a note that you couldn't get, and it was really hard, and then there was another note that you couldn't get because it was too low. And I didn't know some of the notes. I didn't really like that bit. But I liked it when I was actually doing it here with my teacher because it was actually not as hard as I thought. (Clarinet student, eleven years old)

On the other hand, some students enjoyed having the independence to work at home, and many of these came back after a week with surprising results. Some described the kind of detailed work that they were able to do at home, which would be difficult to do in a lesson with the teacher "breathing down your neck."

At home I get to be independent. I can just do it at my own speed, and sometimes I feel I've been pushed a bit too hard in the lessons. (Piano student, eleven years old)

At home I played the CD in really tiny segments and just did each segment, and then also I did some of just playing it over and over again and just picking up on it. And I kind of gave myself time to work out the notes and everything, and work out like that tiny bit, whether it was three or four notes, and then move on onto the next bit. (Cello student, fifteen years old)

I played like a couple of notes and then sung it to myself with playing notes, trying to get the similar one, and then when I thought I had it, I would play the whole thing with it to see if it actually sounded the same. Put the CD on, and then play a couple of notes from the CD, like listen to a couple of notes, stop the CD, and try to get the same ones and then when I thought I had achieved how to play with the CD, go on to the next couple of notes. (Saxophone student, fifteen years old)

## Equipment needed for home practice

If students wish to practice at home, they will need a means of audio-reproduction in the room where they practice.

## Which students can take part?

The strategies can be adopted by any learner at any level from near-beginner to advanced. The exact point at which a beginner can start will depend partly on the instrument. For example, a complete beginner on the piano can tackle the tasks more readily, but for brass, bowed string, and woodwind instruments a basic ability to create pitches is advised in most cases. In general, experience of approximately one- to two-year's instrumental tuition is recommended as a prerequisite, but as with all aspects this is up to the teacher's professional judgement. More advanced players will approach the tasks at their own level, right up to diploma standard and beyond.

## What kinds of backgrounds do teachers need?

The strategies can be used by instrumental teachers from any background. They were designed for classically trained teachers and particularly for those who may lack confidence or experience in ear-playing; however, the strategies have also been found useful by teachers who had backgrounds in informal learning, popular and folk music, and professional ear-playing experience in music theatre.

## Teacher preparation

If you want your students to practice at home, you will either need to give them the handbook's website URL and password so they can access the tracks, or make an electronic copy of the chosen tracks for each student. How exactly a copy is to be made will vary depending on the available technology; since this is likely to change rapidly I have refrained from recommending particular software, websites, and the like here. If you wish to make the copies on CD, both popular-style pieces and all their tracks will fit onto one CD, and the classical pieces and tracks onto another.

You will also need to give your students a track list so they can find the track(s) they wish to work on. A printable track list is available on the handbook's website.

If you wish to use the materials only during lesson time, then you just need one copy of the audio tracks to be available in your teaching room.

Some instrumental teachers may wish to learn to play the tracks by ear themselves before the lessons start, or depending on your experience you may prefer to pick them up during the lessons. Notation of the music has not been provided, because it is important that the teacher engages in the same aural experience as the students.

## Notions of "correctness" and "incorrectness," "wrong" and "right"

I use the terms "correctness," "incorrectness," "wrong," and "right" throughout this handbook advisedly. What might be considered "wrong" in a notational context might, in the context of the approaches taken here, be considered adequate, or as a creative, improvisatory embellishment which is to be encouraged. The reasons for this are complex and how a judgement is made will depend on the teacher, the task in hand and the needs of individual learners.

## How does this differ from the Suzuki method?

In common with the Suzuki method, this approach places central emphasis on learning by listening to and copying recordings. However, the two methods derive from different starting points, have different aims, teaching-and-learning strategies, and lead towards different outcomes. The main differences are these:

- In the Hear, Listen, Play approach each piece is not specially designed for the student's particular instrument. Rather, the student is required to adapt the music for their own instrument, which may involve putting it up or down an octave or two.

- The pieces are not graded or differentiated according to a systematic notion of students' ability or expected progress. Rather, the same pieces are given to all students regardless of their level, and each student finds her own way through the task.

- The role of the teacher is explained in detail later in this handbook. It differs from that of the Suzuki teacher in that the student is encouraged to direct their own learning to a much greater extent. In addition, unlike with the Suzuki method, no formal involvement of the parent is required.

- The able student may wish to seek a perfect, correct replication of what is on the recording. In many cases, though, it is more appropriate to achieve an approximation before moving on. A free, improvisatory approach and interpretation of the music is encouraged for all students. Many will start to improvise during the learning of the track; others will learn it note-for-note first and then start to improvise spontaneously.

- After only five or six sessions or fewer, the student is given free choice about what music to play.

Photo © David Baker
as part of the Ear
Playing Project,
http://earplaying
.ioe.ac.uk

# HeLP in instrumental settings: the basic steps

Teachers may wish to combine the stages in a variety of ways. Option A is the basic rec-ommended approach; please see the flowcharts in section 4, which illustrate this option and a few other possible options.

## Stage 1: Popular styles

For the instrumental setting in Option A, teachers begin in stage 1 with one or both of the given popular-style pieces. These are "Dreaming" (track 1 for C instruments, or track 11 for B-flat instruments if you prefer); or "Link Up" (track 21). The reason for choosing this style of music is that it is designed around short, repeated motives or riffs, which provides a simple starting point for the task.

- Firstly, explain to the student that they are going to learn to play some music by ear.

- Together, listen to your pre-chosen piece, or listen with the student to both pieces and have them choose one.

- Play the next track of the chosen piece, which will be the bass riff on its own, repeated over and over for two minutes. *Whilst the track is playing* ask the student to listen and try to find and play any of the notes they can hear.

- Tell them they may want to play the music in a different octave to that on the recording, depending on their instrument.

- Tell them that it doesn't matter if they make mistakes, and that this is not a test.

- Let them attempt to find notes whilst the recording plays.

- Give them time; allow them to learn by trial and error; encourage them; avoid criticisms.

- Observe what they do for a couple of minutes: it is important that you let the recording continue to play and do not switch it off, even if the student is not playing.

Once two or more tracks have been learnt in this way, (see below for how this may hap-pen and how you can help), the student should be asked to attempt to switch smoothly from one riff to another, ideally without dropping a beat. Once this is mastered to a point which your judgement suggests is adequate, they can improvise their own "arrangement," by putting the riffs together in any order, or by creating their own versions of the riffs and then putting them together, and so on.

It is important to bear in mind that the riffs become more technically demanding as they progress through the track numbers. In "Dreaming," for example, the final two vibraphone parts will be beyond many learners; in "Link Up," the violin "twiddle" and the main melody are likely to be too difficult for some. It is fine to simply use whatever tracks are accessible for each learner, starting with the easiest ones first and altogether leaving out those that are too difficult. As with all steps of HeLP, the teacher's judgement is crucial, so that learners are sufficiently challenged but not threatened. More suggestions about this are given below.

The riffs can be played along to the recording, in a duet with the teacher, as a group with other students, or any of these. For pianists or other keyboardists you will want them to learn a right-hand part and a left-hand part, before playing with both hands. If this proves too difficult for some of the less experienced students, it is a good idea to simplify the bass part for them: for example, they can try just playing a pulse on one note. This will free up hand coordination and can lead to increased ability to play with two hands in the next stages.

At the end of the first session, most teachers are likely to want to give the student a copy of the audio tracks either on a CD or by some other means, and ask them to continue learning the music at home, just as we do with notated music. Again, just as with notation, some students will work hard at the task and improve; others will not do any practice; and others may get frustrated when attempting the task on their own and may prefer to do it only during the lesson. Either is fine.

It is likely that you and the student will feel three to five sessions are all that is needed on either popular-style piece before moving on to the next one, or on to stage 2.

## Stage 2: Classical pieces

Stage 2 begins around the third or fourth lesson for most students. It involves classical music, which is constructed in longer-breathed and therefore more challenging phrasing.

On the audio recording, each piece is played first in its complete instrumentation; then in a two-part version, slightly simplified in some cases; then in single parts, phrase by phrase, repeated over and over for two minutes, as indicated in the track listings in appendix E.

- First, listen together to the openings (only) of the six full pieces of classical music (Mozart, Beethoven, Clara Schumann, Handel, Brahms and Bach, tracks 28, 34, 40, 44, 52, and 58 respectively).

- Ask the student to choose one piece. If they express no preference, suggest one that you think would be suitable for them. However, if they have a strong preference, it is important that their choice comes before yours, even if you think a different piece would be more suitable. Later, once they have tried the piece they chose, they may wish to take your advice and try a more accessible one.

- Together, listen to the two-part version; then listen to a track with the repeated single part, choosing either melody or bass according to preference.

- As with stage 1, allow the student to attempt to pick out pitches, transposing up or down an octave if necessary, whilst the chosen single-line version plays on the recording; and refer to the teaching strategies in section 6 for ways to support them.

Once the line is mastered or nearly mastered, the student can, for example, play the melody over the recorded bass track, or play the bass track along with the melody; or play in a duet with the teacher or other students. Again, ideally, pianists will play with both hands, even if one of the parts needs to be simplified by the teacher.

## Stage 3: Free choice

Stage 3 can begin whenever you and the student wish. If you follow the stages as set out here—that is, you attempt one piece during stage 1 and one piece during stage 2—then stage 3 is likely to come around the fifth to the seventh lesson for most students.

This is the point at which the practice of informal learning, as distinct from just ear-playing, is accessed more fully because the student is given free choice about which music to learn. The aim is to increase enjoyment and motivation, and to open up the world of music for students to adapt chosen pieces for their own instrument and skill level.

- In preparation, the student is requested to listen to their own selection of music, away from the lesson, and choose any piece they like. It can be in any style and for any instrument or combination of instruments, including voice. Some students are likely to choose music composed for their particular instrument; others will choose music played by totally different instruments or that is sung; some are likely to bring film music, others classical music, and others a variety of popular musics. The main issue is that the music should be the students' own choice.

- They then bring a recording of the piece to the next lesson, either in MP3 format, on CD, or via some other method. Our experience has been that most students bring music in MP3 format, meaning that iPod speakers, a computer, or other digital-sound-reproduction equipment are needed, so that both student and teacher can listen to the music together.

- Those students who are comfortable working with aural-learning strategies on their own at home can start teaching themselves to play any part of their chosen piece they wish, by ear. Students then come to the lesson and show the teacher what they have done, and together you work on the music, using strategies as for the other stages, described below. For students who want constant teacher support, the learning can all be done inside lesson time.

# Possible combinations and orders of stages: instrumental tuition

The following flowchart illustrates the stages as they are described in the previous sections along with some other possible combinations.

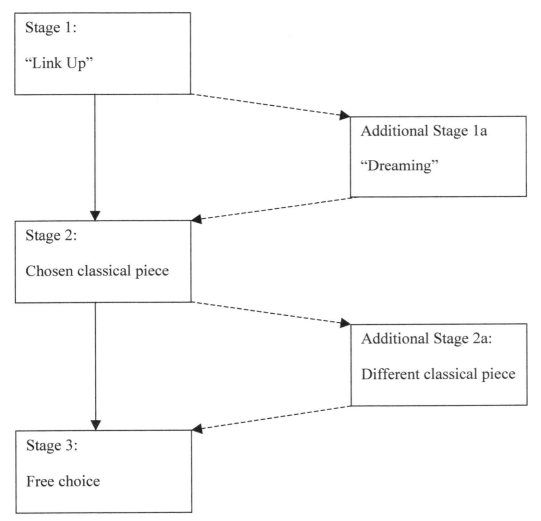

**Figure 1**
Option A: instrumental tuition

**Figure 2**
Option B: instrumental tuition (possibly for a fast learner or a more advanced student)

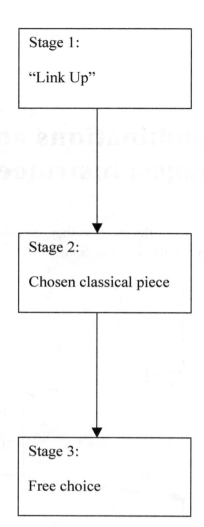

```
┌─────────────────────────┐
│ Stage 1:                │
│                         │
│ "Link Up"               │
│                         │
└─────────────────────────┘
             │
             ▼
┌─────────────────────────┐
│ Stage 2:                │
│                         │
│ "Dreaming"              │
│                         │
└─────────────────────────┘
             │
             ▼
┌─────────────────────────┐
│ Stage 3:                │
│                         │
│ Free choice             │
│                         │
└─────────────────────────┘
```

**Figure 3**

Option C: instrumental tuition (possibly for a learner who is not studying classical music)

Clearly there are many other possible ways of combining the stages. Some teachers may wish to do only one stage, which, depending on their judgement and their students' needs, could be any one of the several. The above are merely some suggestions.

18

# 5

# How are students likely to respond?

Each student will approach the task in their own way. However, our research suggests that you are likely to witness four main "learning styles," which are discernable at the very outset. These are not fixed by rigid boundaries but are fluid examples of the students' initial, spontaneous responses. They occur naturally in the sense that they are not the result of prior teaching. We found in the research that hardly any students had ever tried to do this before, so the responses are also unlikely to be the result of prior learning. Not every student will fit neatly into one of the learning styles, and most students will pass through more than one learning style as time goes by. Nonetheless, we have found it is both interesting and useful to identify these learning styles, particularly in relation to the very first responses and attempts made at the task by students. If as teachers we understand our students better, we can be more open and responsive to their individual strengths and needs.

## Learning styles

1. The "impulsive learning style" in the instrumental setting.

   The student may start to play impulsively or loudly without apparently listening; they may or may not play correct pitches or rhythms; they may quite soon fix on their own version of the riff and stick to it without seeming to check whether it is correct, that is, exactly the same as the recording. It is helpful to encourage such students to play, to let the music flow, and to help them to feel confident in what they are doing, rather than insisting they get the notes right.

2. The "practical learning style" in the instrumental setting.

   The student may listen carefully, then quietly play up or down a scale, or play notes in some systematic way, apparently intending to find a note that sounds right. Once such a note has been found, they are likely to soon recognise it, return to it, and use it as an anchor from which to seek other notes. Students with this learning style may well be able to pick up five or six riffs within ten minutes, depending on their age, instrument, and experience.

3. The "shot-in-the-dark learning style" in the instrumental setting.

   The student may appear completely thrown by the task, and very hesitant to play a note at all. They may seem anxious or afraid to play something that they think is wrong. They are likely to stab at isolated pitches, and even if they play a correct note, they may not recognise it as such. Such students may find it very difficult to play anything at all, and your guidance will be needed at an earlier stage than with learners exhibiting the impulsive or practical approaches described earlier. A huge amount of encouragement is also required, and constant reminders that it doesn't matter if the student plays a wrong note or a note that is different from the recording.

4. The "theoretical approach" in the instrumental setting.

The student may ask a lot of questions. Some of these may be related to clarifying the task, such as "Do you mean I can start playing now?" or "I don't understand what to do." When such clarification is still needed, the task has not yet begun properly. The theoretical approach occurs after clarification, if and when the student asks questions about the music itself. These might include questions such as "Are there three notes?" "Is the first note the same as the second?" "Is it the same note three times?" Of course, any such questions should be answered, and again, some other guidance from you may be needed at an earlier stage than with impulsive or practical students.

## Pitch and rhythm in the instrumental setting

Cutting across these four learning styles you will be likely to witness different approaches and responses to pitch and to rhythm.

### Pitch

A small number of learners will display signs of so-called perfect pitch or absolute pitch. This usually manifests itself by going immediately to the correct note without any trial-and-error. However, amongst these, some students will recognise the note immediately and use it as an anchor to seek other notes, whilst others may not appear to recognise it as correct at all. In the latter case, it may be that playing the correct note was merely a coincidence; or it may be that knowledge of the note is somehow deeply buried in the learner's subconscious mind, and it was just confidence in that knowledge which was lacking. Learners displaying signs of perfect pitch are likely to be spread across all four of the learning styles identified above.

### Rhythm

Some learners, including many who do not play correct pitches may nonetheless display an excellent rhythmic sense and be able to play accurately in time with the recording from the outset. Others will falter and be unable to keep going.

## Other possible learning styles

You may notice other learning styles that we did not come across or that we did not spot. Also, some learners may have been spontaneously applying previous knowledge, either from music theory or from pieces they had already played; or evidencing other responses.

## From learning style to learning strategy in the instrumental setting

Although some students will begin by exhibiting one or more of the learning styles, it is highly likely that, given encouragement, all of them will improve at the task as time goes by. Many who start off by taking shots in the dark, for example, will gradually become more attuned to the task and begin to develop strategies by which to help themselves. These could include using an anchor note from which to seek other notes, listening more carefully, or playing up and down scalar patterns to find notes. Also, many of those who start off as impulsive, shot-in-the-dark, or practical learners may gradually become more akin to the theoretical learners and thus ask more and more questions. As this occurs, what may have started out as a spontaneous learning style slowly matures into a variety of acquired learning strategies.

21

Photo © David Baker
as part of the Ear
Playing Project,
http://earplaying
.ioe.ac.uk

# Teaching strategies: the role of the teacher in instrumental settings

One of the reasons for identifying the different learning styles is that it can enable teachers to understand differences between students and thus to respond appropriately to the learning style of each individual. Furthermore, it can open our eyes and ears to approaches that might be different to the way we ourselves learnt. Thus it can challenge our own immediate assumptions, which are likely to be based in some remote way upon our own natural learning style, whether or not we are conscious of the fact.

It is important that teachers start off by observing the behaviours and responses of their students, and by giving them time to work out the pitches themselves, without the teacher jumping straight in and telling them. Some teachers have expressed an initial fear that by standing back more than usual, they will not be doing their job. Once they have tried the strategies, though, they usually find that by standing back they are still teaching, but in a different way. In the words of some of those on the receiving end—the instrumental students:

> Well I guess the teacher is there to help you. To get you to improve the song, but it might actually be counterproductive to actually *tell* the student how to do it. . . . I guess if you are struggling with a note and the teacher tells you it, then that's one note you weren't able to figure out yourself, and that's one note in the future—well not that particular note—but that's one thing you might not be able to do in the future. If you are left to actually have to work out yourself, then you are obviously going to be better, but it might take you longer to learn the piece. I think the teacher is probably, rather than teaching you the notes, probably better to teach you *how to work out* the notes. (Piano student, seventeen years old)

> I think it's a good idea to find most of the notes on my own because, if I had help from my teacher, 'cause otherwise I'd hadn't have learnt anything. (Piano student, ten years old)

> I think it's a good idea to make you find the notes by yourself because it's challenging and it's like how you learn. It's like learning. (Piano student, eight years old)

> I think it was a good idea to try to figure them out by myself 'cause, if she told me the notes, then I'd have just done it and I wouldn't actually be teaching myself to do it. (Piano student, eleven years old)

I think it was a good idea to make us find most of the notes on our own, but I think that also we need, like, a bit of help, like if we get really stuck we might need to know where it is roughly. (Clarinet student, nine years old)

I think it was a good idea to figure them out 'cause, even though it took long to figure them out, it's good to do it yourself so that you can progress more . . . I think it's not bad if they tell you the notes but I'd say that I wouldn't progress as far if I kept getting told the notes. (Piano student, thirteen years old)

Students should be working at a level that is both sufficiently challenging and sufficiently approachable. This involves a careful balance, which can only be up to your professional judgement. It means that some students will play only the first two or three riffs before you move on to stage 2; others will play each riff only inaccurately before moving on to the next riff; whilst others can be encouraged to play all the riffs quite accurately. No written formula can replace the judgement and intuition of the teacher in knowing where and when to move forward or to pause for improvement.

Teachers should not necessarily ask students to seek perfection. For some students, particularly those who are confident and who have good pitch and rhythmic sense, it may well be appropriate to aim for a high level of accuracy. For others, though, too much insistence on accuracy is liable to induce boredom, lack of confidence, or frustration. For such students, rather than perfection, an approximation of the riff is more suitable, enough to allow them to keep the flow of the music going and to play along, even if it is in their own way. Encouragement is needed above all else.

Furthermore, the whole question of what is correct and what is incorrect is challenged by this exercise; and it is here that the beginnings of improvisation are born. You are likely to find an interesting question mark over what counts as a mistake and what counts as an embellishment or improvisatory idea. If a student is playing in time but without accurate pitch, for example, you may decide to move on rather than stop to correct what they are doing: perhaps what they are playing "works"; perhaps it can be considered an improvisatory embellishment rather than a mistake. Both accuracy and improvisatory ability will improve as time goes by.

Below are two "fly-on-the-wall" examples, slightly edited, and chosen from amongst the 228 lessons that we observed. These provide typical illustrations of how the teacher can step in to offer help without destroying the aural nature of the task or the expression of the student's individual learning style.

The first example is from the first lesson of stage 2, copying the Brahms melody A, with a fifteen-year-old saxophone student who had initially been categorised in the shot-in-the-dark learning style.

### EX. 1: HELPING BY SINGING

*Teacher:* Right. It's track 64. Are you ready? Should I just put it on?

*Shilpa:* OK.

*Teacher:* And see how you can get on. (1:29 music starts. Shilpa plays along with the Brahms melody A; she lets it play for one rendition, then joins in; her saxophone is a bit out of tune; she stumbles after the first few notes, when she gets to the quavers (eighth notes); then picks up halfway through, stumbles again, then picks up the opening and stumbles again. Basically she knows the first notes; finally though she gets through the first half of the phrase.)

*Shilpa:* Sorry.

*Teacher:* Don't worry. (Shilpa plays correctly). That's really fantastic, let's just stop there (2:41 music stops) and tune a bit, because you are a bit sharp I think, aren't you? Do you want to just—you've got to tune to this, so push the mouthpiece in a bit, and see if that helps a bit. That's really great work actually. Let's try it again now, from the start (3:00 music starts. Shilpa is more in tune. She starts and stumbles but picks up again and stumbles again).

*Teacher:* It's just that bit that is foxing you. (3:33 music stops). You get it on the second phrase. So the first phrase goes (the teacher sings, Shilpa plays along to the teacher's singing, which slows the music down, then Shilpa gets it.) That's it. And then the second phrase. (The teacher sings the second phrase.) It's just a slightly different pattern, and the first one is, if you remember (teacher sings). It's that bit. (Shilpa plays). That's it, let's put it on again (4:06 track starts; she plays along perfectly now for several renditions, having had that little bit of help.) It's really, really good. (Shilpa plays. 4:54 music stops). That's fantastic. You've done it all by yourself. Really, really good. Now did you say you'd had a look at the following track? That's incredible. Right, let's have a go at that and see where the problems come in. (5:06, music starts. Shilpa plays along to the first few notes, then stumbles at the larger interval.)

*Shilpa:* I think that's where it is.

*Teacher:* Is it there?

*Shilpa:* Yes.

*Teacher:* Right so (5:24, music stops. The teacher sings the part). Play along with my singing. (Shilpa plays following the teacher who is slowly singing the phrase note by note). That's it. Right; let's do that again with me singing, because I can slow it down. (Shilpa plays following the teacher singing, note by note). That's it. Yes, just go (Shilpa plays following the singing note by note) and again.

*Teacher:* I am losing it myself now. You've kind of felt everything there, you don't know exactly but it was working, so let's put it back on and see how you go with playing along. (7:39 music starts. Shilpa plays along, stumbles). OK, just remind yourself of that (7:58 music stops). Sorry I forgot what track that was. (The teacher sings). Track 54. OK, ready for it now? (8:17, track 54 starts. She plays right from the start, getting quite a lot of notes but not all.) That's really hard. Try it again next time it comes around. (Shilpa plays again, practicing bits by doing it *after* it's just played.) Well done, well done. Now see if you can get it this time. (Shilpa plays). You are nearly there (9:50 music stops). I think you can cope with that at home now, don't you? I think you can, and then what you could do, what would be really nice is, if next time, you've got two weeks now, I'd like you to play the whole of that melody and to join it up. You just need to listen to the full one, or the two-part one, the full one is probably nicer, and play along so that you join both melody A and melody B together.

*Shilpa:* OK.

*Teacher:* And if you don't manage to get every single note, don't worry, what would be lovely, is to hear a really nice performance of the whole melody, with good tonguing, phrasing, good breathing and all that.

In this example the teacher is:

• Advising on tuning.

• Singing the pitches individually, waiting for the student to find each sung pitch, then singing the next one.

• Giving encouragement and moving on to the next track even though the first one is not perfect, so as to keep going and not get stuck on one aspect of the task.

• Setting a homework task.

• Advising on how technical aspects can later be brought into the activity.

The next example, this time with a thirteen-year-old trombonist, is drawn from the sixth project lesson, which happens to be the first lesson of stage 3, where the student has brought his own music to copy—"Monster Mash" by Madness. This student was also categorised in the shot-in-the-dark learning style at the outset and was so hesitant in the first lesson that he hardly played a note for two minutes and had to be encouraged to try. He later expressed having felt a great deal of trepidation about the task but said, as many other students did, that it turned out to be easier than he expected. It is worth noticing that he is beginning, by the time of this lesson, to ask a lot of questions, thus moving from a shot-in-the-dark to a theoretical learning style.

### EX. 2: HELPING BY SINGING AND LINKING THE MUSIC

*Teacher:* That's it, now could you bear that in mind? That's a C. OK, so (the teacher sings C–E-flat–G; Oliver plays C–D–E). OK, look the next note—what scales do you know on the trombone?

*Oliver:* B flat major, C major, C minor, D minor—

*Teacher:* Fine, fine, fine. Play me a C-minor scale. (Oliver plays the first five notes of a C-minor scale). Just those five notes. Did you hear them? (The teacher sings.) Play them again. Right, now, the tune has got three of those notes in it.

*Oliver:* Is it the first three?

*Teacher:* No. The first three are (the teacher sings C–D–E-flat).

*Oliver:* Is it the first two and then skip to the fourth? One, three, four?

*Teacher:* Yes, it's one, three, but not four.

*Oliver:* One, three, five?.

*Teacher:* Yes, one, three, five! It's very common you know. Any time you hear that sort of thing, (singing) then it's going to be one, three, five. So (the teacher plays on the piano. Oliver plays). Good, do it again. (Oliver plays) and then (the teacher sings). Can you hear what those are?

*Oliver:* It starts the same as the fifth on this, doesn't it? I can't remember.

*Teacher:* (The teacher sings). Two different notes. Yes. (The teacher sings). You are getting it. And the last note. (The teacher sings. Oliver repeats). You are getting it. You are getting the idea as well, about how to work it out. See if you can play the whole thing now. (Oliver plays). Nearly, nearly, nearly. (The teacher sings). So it does that bit twice. Yes, you put an extra note in there, that's not in the tune, but otherwise it was fine. Try it again. (Oliver plays) Again (the teacher sings), just do that. (Oliver plays) and then (the teacher sings, Oliver repeats). No, it doesn't start on the same pitch, it starts on the note below. (The teacher sings, Oliver repeats). And then it's just (the teacher sings, Oliver repeats and gets the whole melody, without the audio recording). Yes. That's it. Do that three times. (Oliver plays) and again (Oliver plays) and again (Oliver plays). That's brilliant. Let's put the CD on, and see if you can play when it comes on.

Here, the teacher is:

- Linking the task to scales which the student already knows.

- Linking the task to theory concerning how triads are built up.

- Asking the student to listen and answer questions about the notes.

- Describing the notes as for example "below" rather than giving away the exact note name.

- Singing in order to help the student find pitches.

- Playing some of the pitches on the piano.

- Giving encouragement.

The following list shows additional points about the above examples approaches, plus other strategies, which can be brought into play, all according to the teacher's professional judgement about the progress and needs of each individual student:

- The teacher can sing the pitches whilst the student plays. In this way it is possible to stop on a sung pitch and hold it until the student finds it; and/or to sing at a slower pace, dwell on particular notes or passages, or stop and repeat short segments.

27

- The teacher can play the pitches on the student's own instrument. This can be done either while the student plays, so you are playing together, or while the student watches, or both. It can be approached in the same way as singing, and can help students who are visual learners and like to watch as well as listen. The immediately visual element will be more prominent for some instruments such as the piano, guitar, or cello, than for others such as the flute or trumpet.

- The teacher can play the riff or melody whilst the recording plays, thus again allowing the student to learn by both listening and watching, but this time the teacher keeps the flow of the music going. The student can then join in as and when he is ready.

- The teacher can stop to show students where to put their fingers, or how to change their embouchures, for example.

- The teacher can seek pitches themselves using a trial-and-error approach, thus enabling the learner to witness how this can be done.

- You may wish to simplify the line so that the student can keep the flow without stumbling over a difficult passage. This is especially helpful in the case of pianists, some of whom may be able to play with two hands only if the bass line is reduced to a series of crotchets (quarter notes) played on one note, for example.

- You may wish to suggest that the student play a particular scale, arpeggio, or chord in order to help them understand the key or the shape of the line.

- You can ask the student to sing the line (if she is comfortable singing), and/or to tap the rhythm.

- It may be helpful to suggest that the student seek notes in a different octave to the one he has chosen.

- You may wish to describe verbally what is happening in the music, for example, "this bit jumps a note," or "This uses notes one, three, and five of the scale."

- Inevitably, rather than suggesting and telling, teachers may want to teach by asking questions. For example, the aforementioned suggestions would turn into questions such as "Can you hear if there's jump in the music; where is it?" "Can you tell me which notes of the scale are used here?" and so on.

- You may wish to give a note name, particularly for the first note of a line, then allow the student to work out the other notes by ear.

- Once the student has found the basic pitches, towards the latter parts of each stage, you will undoubtedly want to offer advice on technique—fingering, breathing, intonation; and musical interpretation—phrasing, dynamics, and so on.

Particularly in stage 3 (free choice), students may select music in difficult or impossible keys for them to play, or which is much too fast for them. If so, they will learn from this experience and can be encouraged or guided to choose a different, more accessible piece next time. Alternatively, you could play the music in a transposition or a simplified version on your own instrument and allow the students to copy from that.

It is important not to tell the student too much, too soon, and to avoid telling them they've got it wrong. They are likely to lose confidence and give up. Students will respond best to encouragement.

**30**

# 7

# What were the overall views of the participants?

## Teachers' views

Overall, the fifty-four teachers from whom we received questionnaire and interview data, as well as others who spoke in meetings or sent emails and blog comments, reported that their confidence increased. Before the project started, 41 percent expressed a lack of confidence in teaching ear-playing and aural skills. At the end of the project, after just a few lessons, this figure had been reduced to 0 percent. Eighty-five percent agreed or strongly agreed with the statement "I have learnt useful teaching skills during the project." Others said they had learnt new perspectives, on the one hand, about how to teach, and on the other hand, about how their students learn:

> *String Teacher:* I found taking part in the whole project really interesting and rewarding. It gave me new insights into how people learn, and has given me new ideas which I will definitely incorporate into future lessons.

> *Piano Teacher:* I am finding this absolutely fascinating; and it's already having an effect on the rest of my teaching too, just in a general way; and it's reminding me that there is more than one way to learn, you know, what a middle C is.

> *Brass Teacher:* I think I've learnt quite a lot. Just mainly to sit back a lot more and let them, you know, have their little time of experimenting. Because it might take a thousand words to explain something, and if they can just hear something, for them to hear it and to try and do it is worth a thousand more words than me trying to verbally explain it.

> *Woodwind Teacher:* Well, I've learnt just generally that I need to get away from prescriptive instrumental teaching.

> *Piano Teacher:* It definitely showed me how quick I am to correct students' mistakes and things like that and how I don't allow them to work out their own problems. I think predominately it showed me a lot about how I am as a teacher, in terms of jumping in and correcting mistakes and wanting to be very hands on, and understanding that it is better for me to sit back and not necessarily do everything for them. Yes, that has been quite an interesting realisation. Yes, that's amazing really.

> *Piano Teacher:* I've learnt to try and make lessons more pupil-centred and not to direct lessons quite so much, and let the pupil learn by their mistakes as opposed

to trying to rectify mistakes, you know, even when you can see that it is just about to happen. It's sort of taking a step back, actually, and sort of letting them get on with it and that's a difficult thing to do.

Ninety-one percent of the teachers stated that they would continue to use the strategies in a general way after the project had finished, and 87 percent agreed that the project would influence the way they teach in the future. One teacher, for example, was creating her own ear-playing audio materials for use before introducing notation of the pieces; another created her own materials for her primary school lunchtime ensemble involving some twenty-five pupils, many of whom were complete beginners. Some teachers felt that they had learnt new and useful aural musicianship techniques for themselves:

*Piano Teacher:* I have been learning the pieces too and have found that working by ear makes you much more aware of the structure of the piece, which is an aid to learning. I have never been able to memorise using the printed score but have been able to do it by listening, albeit playing at a simple level!

*Piano Teacher:* I am really enjoying taking part in the project. It is stretching me musically too, and I have found myself at the piano working things out by ear. It has also stretched me technically!

*Piano Teacher:* I've learnt quite a lot about how to approach things because I had to work it out for myself. I had to do it in order to teach it. So I can now more or less play about five Grade 1 pieces by ear, which I would never have done before. I've done my own recordings. Having to do that and then listening to them, to make sure they are all OK for the students, and then teaching them—I found it's gone in.

Ninety-three percent of the teachers felt that their students had benefited from the ear-playing, and 74 percent stated that the general musicianship of their students had improved. Some teachers, for example, pointed to how students were able to play in a more "musical" way, owing to hearing the music and knowing how it should sound; others found new ways to teach technique:

*Brass Teacher:* I think they were learning bits of technique in a much more musical way than if it was just in a scale book; or if you are reading notation, sometimes it can come out so the notes are all there but it's not remotely phrased how it should be. So in that sense with the ear-playing, you are starting from the musical point of view. So that was good I think, yes. And they were copying things that they heard in the recording, perhaps a short bass stroke or something of that kind, whereas if they were doing that from the notation you'd have to *tell* them.

*Piano Teacher:* I was concerned about getting the best fingering without seeing the score, but this has been an opportunity to get pupils to think about fingering and why we finger in particular ways, and make alterations where necessary.

Eighty percent of the teachers stated that they felt their students' general aural development and listening skills had improved:

*Piano Teacher:* You are getting away from that piece of music on the stand and sort of being a slave to it, and it's encouraging you to use your aural skills.

*Woodwind Teacher:* I think that they have all developed their listening skills totally.

*Piano Teacher:* I have learnt just how positive it is to be free from notation ... and how freeing them from the notation by getting them to play by ear is such a very obvious way of developing their aural skills.

*Piano Teacher:* Ear playing encourages looking at patterns, especially on the piano where patterns can be clearly seen.

Many also believed their students' confidence had increased:

*Woodwind Teacher:* I think a lot of them have gained a bit more confidence on their instruments and what they can do with their instruments, particularly because quite a few of them are using notes that they didn't realise they could get or, you know, or we haven't done yet, which is good for them.

*Piano Teacher:* I think they've learnt that there is more ways of learning things than the ones they have already done before, I think it's given some of them more confidence.

*String Teacher:* I think that one student in particular has learnt that she's actually got very good ears, and perhaps she didn't know before. And she felt very proud of herself, so for her it was a real eye-opener.

*Brass Teacher:* Above all, it's given them confidence and a sense of self-enablement and self-motivation that they can actually go and listen to a piece of music and work it out for themselves. It's like learning to swim. You have to dive in. You have to dive into the water and be prepared to splash around and make a mess. So hopefully that confidence to just try it, it will either be wrong or right, eventually you'll find a way that's right.

Most teachers felt that their students had enjoyed the ear-playing experience:

*Woodwind Teacher:* I think it was a resounding success. That's my comment. It really was! All the teachers enjoyed it and all the students enjoyed it.

*Piano Teacher:* I am so glad that I took part in the project; I am learning to listen better myself as a result, and I definitely feel I have a new way into helping my pupils with developing their aural skills. I also think that learning to play by ear will increase their enjoyment of playing the piano.

## Students' views

Seventy-nine percent of the 193 students who sent questionnaire replies ticked boxes to say they found the project "enjoyable" or "very enjoyable." To my surprise, this included learners who had appeared very hesitant at first, such as both Shilpa and Oliver, parts of whose lessons have been cited earlier. Many of them also told us during interviews that they felt they had in some way expanded their horizons. This was partly in relation to the greater range of music that they now realised was available for them to play, and partly in relation to coming across a new and different way of learning:

> I've learnt that you can play any music you feel comfortable with, and that you can try any type of music you want anytime really. (Trumpet student, fourteen years old)

> I've learnt that music isn't fixed, and I don't have to just plonk a piece of sheet music in front of me and try to do that. I can do a piece that I am interested in, you know, it can be more fun than what I originally thought it would be. I got the notes quicker so, obviously my recognition of them had, you know, improved. (Saxophone student, fifteen years old)

> I learnt that it's enjoyable to learn by ear as well, and a lot of people do that, so it's not like you can't, because a lot of people do that as well. And it's quite fun to do, with the beat and the bass line as well. It's quite fun. (Clarinet student, thirteen years old)

> I am happy to admit that I enjoyed it a lot more than normal like, exams and learning from notation. I enjoy trying to pick it out yourself and working out for yourself rather than it, it's not like it's been given to you, but it is more of a sense of you actually knowing the piece, being your own piece once you've picked out. So I'd say, I enjoyed it a bit more than learning from paper and notation in general. (Piano student, seventeen years old)

Seventy-two percent of the students reported that before the project they had never done ear-playing of a similar kind, that is, from an audio recording. Yet, having done the project, 80 percent thought that playing by ear was "important" or "very important," and 80 percent also said they would prefer to learn to play by ear as well as by notation, rather than by one of those means only.

We also observed a large shift in the perceived difficulty level of the task. Prior to experience through the project materials, 55 percent of the students thought ear playing would be "difficult" or "very difficult":

> I thought it would be quite difficult because I am used to, sort of, looking at the music and I am playing that, but I've done, I've hardly done any of that CD thing before, and I haven't got a very good memory. (Saxophone student, eleven years old)

> I thought it would take me a long time because I've never done anything like that before. I'm used to having it always written out and in front of me so that I can, yeah, look at it. (Piano student, thirteen years old)

> I was a tiny bit worried because I didn't really play without notes. (Piano student, ten years old)

> My first thought was: "This isn't going to happen, at all!" (Trombone student, thirteen years old)

However, after working through the project materials, only 12 percent of the students remarked that the task in fact turned out to be "difficult" or "very difficult," whilst 54 percent deemed it of "medium difficulty" and 33 percent found it "easy" or "very easy." This is important because it suggests that instrumental students may tend to regard ear-playing as something unapproachable; and yet, being given an opportunity and the encouragement to try it, they—and their teachers—are likely to discover that it is in fact very approachable as well as enjoyable. In this way we are giving them not only a musical skill in itself but a way of learning, which students can take with them through life if they so wish:

> I've learnt that it's not actually incredibly hard to play by ear. It is possible. (Violin student, twelve years old)

> Well, there are so many different things that I found interesting, and I guess, I think I learnt that it is possible to just play with only listening and not [notated] music as well. And I learnt it's easier than I thought it would be. And I learnt about the way that I play the cello and the methods that I found useful as well because, I mean I knew them roughly before, but this consolidated like all the, all my kind of personal techniques and things that I, yes, I think I've learnt about how to play the cello, that's what I am trying to say. (Cello student, fifteen years old)

> Well, this is much easier and it's also more funner. Certainly this is a lot easier than sight-reading! (Piano student, thirteen years old)

> When I was told about the project I thought it was good, I thought it would be quite nice to try and learn something by ear. I find it easier when I play by ear. I get confused when I play by reading. (Clarinet student, thirteen years old)

Some students described the process of how their views had changed in this respect during the course of the lessons:

> I didn't think it would be impossible because I've seen people do it before but I thought it would be hard and it turned out to be okay, sort of in the middle. I think I just thought, 'cause I've only seen people that are really good on piano do it. I thought it was something that would come with practice on the piano after like ages, and it turns out that it's not. (Piano student, thirteen years old)

> I thought it was going to be quite hard when I first listened to it and, then, once I started going, it was really easy. I thought it was going to be hard because the pieces they sounded really difficult but, when you play them in steps, it's quite easy. (Piano student, eight years old)

> At first, I couldn't really do it because I wasn't really doing it properly and I was getting a bit like annoyed with myself. But, then, as I got better at it, I found it was actually getting quite fun. (Piano student, eleven years old)

Many students reported being surprised at how easy they found the task and also discovering they had latent ear-playing skills of which they had previously been unaware:

> I didn't really ever expect to be able to fully play it like I can do now. Before, I have picked out tunes before by ear—very simple tunes—but I didn't expect to

be able to achieve what I did. I think I can play it quite well now. But I didn't expect to be able to play it like that. I just thought that I'd be able to pick out a few notes here and there. Considering I've been learning notation since I was younger, and this is the first time I've done it by ear, I am sure that the more I did by ear the faster I'd be able to pick it out. I'd probably imagine if I've been doing both since when I actually started piano my ear would be slightly faster, slightly better. (Piano student, seventeen years old)

Some students indicated that the skills they developed helped them in the early stages of learning a new piece:

It helped with learning pieces like the first time. (Piano student, ten years old)

Now, when I have to play music from notation, if I'm just sight reading, I'll kind of know what it's meant to sound like. (Piano student, thirteen years old)

Well, recently, when I started my Grade 4 [intermediate level] exam, 'cause I need it for school, and it was like before, a Grade 4 piece would have probably taken me quite a while to learn 'cause I would have found it difficult. But I picked it up within two or three weeks so like my teacher said that it helped and it did, because she plays it for me before and, then, once you know what it sounds like, you can just kind of know what the kind of rhythm and round about what pitch it is and everything. (Piano student, thirteen years old)

Now, I kind of try and picture maybe where the notes are that's playing in the background on the piano. It's like a piano in my head and I'm thinking "Maybe that's a B." (Piano student, thirteen years old)

Increased sensitivity whilst listening and a better understanding of how music is put together were mentioned by a number of students too:

I'm sort of listening to the actual notes a bit more, like before I was sort of listening to "Oh that's a high note, that's a low note" and now I sort of think "Maybe that's a G, or that's more of an E" or something. (Euphonium student, twelve years old)

I find it really useful to learn by ear, and I pick up on things so much more quickly and I understand the music if I listen to it, whereas if it's just notes on a page, then I don't find it easy to get the gist of it. (Cello student, fifteen years old)

When I listen to a note that's being played, before, if I hadn't have done this thing, then I wouldn't have probably found it, but now, I probably know, I probably find it easier to find the note. (Piano student, ten years old)

I've learnt how to train my ear. I've learnt how to make out parts of the music, how to break it down and how to find notes and how to decipher pitches and understand the beat and the timing and that sort of thing. (Cello student, fourteen years old)

I learnt about using your ears. It's quite important, because it improves a lot of skills and it is quite enjoyable not having to read notes all the time. (Clarinet student, thirteen years old)

I notice kind of different, like the bass and the theme coming, the different kind of sections coming in more than I did before. (Piano student, fourteen years old)

I realise that there's a piece of music being played and it's just repeated through-out the whole song over and over again. And I'm starting to realise that much more now so … I think I have paid attention to that. (Piano student, seventeen years old)

I think "I've heard that before." Well, "I've heard that when I was playing that before" and then I go home and I try to play it and I get a rough idea of what it is sometimes. (Piano student, ten years old)

Well, I just know what instruments are playing, something like that, and their beats and things. (Flute student, ten years old)

Some students reported, without having been asked, that they felt the strategies had helped, or would help them in the aural part of their instrumental grade exam:

Well, I think one of the reasons I got Distinction in my exam is because the project really helped with my aural. At first, I was hitting lots of the wrong notes, then I couldn't hear that I was hitting the wrong notes, but now, I know that I've hit the wrong note and I know if it's the right note as well. (Piano student, eleven years old)

I really thought it helped my aural tests in the exam and I'm really glad I did it. (Piano student, eleven years old)

I wouldn't say the project was like my favourite thing but it's not the worst either 'cause I can see it will help my aural like when I do my exams. (Piano student, thirteen years old)

38

# PART 2

# HeLP in ensemble settings: bands, orchestras, and other groups

Photo © David Baker as part of the Ear Playing Project, http://earplaying .ioe.ac.uk

# Introduction

## The aims of HeLP in ensemble settings are:

- To show ensemble members some basic steps involved in ear-playing, which they may not otherwise come across, based on popular musicians' informal learning practices.

- To enhance students' enjoyment of music making and learning in a variety of ways.

- To enhance students' listening skills in ensemble settings, particularly how well they listen to each other and to their own part within an ensemble.

- To increase students' pitch sense and rhythmic sense.

- To give simple strategies to ensemble leaders and teachers, particularly those who may not be familiar with ear-playing or informal learning.

- To enhance the confidence of teachers in using aural methods in ensemble settings.

- To give teachers insights into aspects of their students' musicality, of which they may have previously been unaware.

## Who participated in the ensemble research, and on which instruments?

Some of the instrumental teachers who took part in the Ear Playing Project <http://earplaying.ioe.ac.uk> described in part 1, worked both as one-to-one instrumental teachers, and also had roles in schools directing larger ensembles. I had designed the HeLP strategies for the instrumental lesson (and the classroom, see part 3), and I had not expected anyone to be interested in taking the strategies into their teacher-directed ensemble work. However, some of the teachers who worked across both these spheres immediately grasped the potential of using the strategies with ensembles. One teacher used the approach for a year with her adult beginner string class, who were taking a course in aural skills; another used the approach with six ensembles across four schools involving students aged six to sixteen. In another school, three instrumental teachers of wind, brass, and strings respectively were all involved in one-to-one HeLP instruction, and they decided to use the strategies across the school. They taught their students, aged eleven to sixteen, to play riffs by ear from "Link Up" (on the handbook's website), in separate lessons. Then they brought all the students together and added a three-piece rock band of older students. The result was a performance at the end-of-year concert, involving thirty-five students playing brass, wind, and bowed strings in an ensemble, by ear, along with support from bass, drums, and electric guitar. One of our teachers used the strategies successfully in scat singing with his choir. We also organised a day for seven blind and visually impaired children who learnt "Link Up" as an ensemble, through the auspices of the Royal National Institute for Blind People (RNIB). Overall, during our research, HeLP was used with:

- An adult-learner string class involving fourteen students.

- Six guitar ensembles.

- Seven other ensembles across four teachers, involving a range of orchestral instruments, rock instruments, recorders, ukuleles, glockenspiels, keyboards, and percussion, with students aged seven to eighteen.

- A group of blind and visually-impaired children in collaboration with the Royal National Institute for Blind People (RNIB)

- A mixed group containing hearing and hearing-impaired children.

- A jazz choir with students aged fifteen to eighteen.

- Thirteen teacher-induction sessions involving a whole-group exercise and small break-out groups with altogether more than two hundred and fifty music teachers. Most of them were instrumental teachers, but some were teacher-educators and classroom teachers. Ten of the sessions took place in the UK, one in Brazil, one in Argentina, and one in Singapore.

In addition, since the research phase the strategies have been used successfully with a group of forty music undergraduates playing instruments ranging from woodwind, bowed strings, and brass to xylophones, a bass guitar, and a harp.

In the research, we collected data by:

- Observations of four band rehearsals, six guitar ensembles, the RNIB day, which was directed by the author, one school concert performance, and one adult string class.

- An interview and a weekly diary written by the adult string teacher across one whole year.

- Interviews with one of the ensemble teachers.

- Questionnaires from the adult string learners and from ninety-four teachers who used the strategies in large ensembles and small groups working with their peers on induction days.

- Participant-observations and informal verbal feedback from the thirteen groups of teachers who used the strategies in practical whole-group and small-group sessions.

Photo © David Baker
as part of the Ear
Playing Project,
http://earplaying
.ioe.ac.uk

# 9

# HeLP in ensemble settings: preliminary practicalities

## Audio materials

For an explanation of what is contained in the audio materials please refer to Note on the Text: "The audio-materials: an overview" (xx) and appendix E, which contains a complete track listing. This is also shown on the handbook's website.

For HeLP in ensemble settings, the popular-style pieces are best. It is recommended to start with "Dreaming" then move on to "Link Up," but this is entirely dependent on your judgement and the age and experience of your students. Within each piece the riffs get progressively more demanding, and it is important that you do not feel the need to necessarily tackle all of them with all the students.

Once familiar with the strategies and the nature of the audio materials, teachers may wish to create their own specially tailored materials. You can also slow down the given tracks, or change their keys using a range of freely available software, if you wish to do so. The main characteristic of the materials, which is important to replicate, is that each part should involve a riff of two to four bars, and should be played continuously for about two minutes. This gives the students enough time to hear what is going on, try out notes, use notes as anchors, and keep on trying. It is best to try out the given materials yourself first so as to fully understand how they function.

## The time frame

Some teachers may wish to use HeLP for the whole of a practice session; others may wish to incorporate the strategies into part of a weekly session. Ideally the sessions should be at least once a week.

## Which instruments can be used?

Any instruments can be used. If you are leading an ensemble with a mix of B-flat, E-flat, and C instruments, you may wish to make a decision as to whether to use the B-flat versions or the C versions provided on the website, or to make other versions yourself in different keys using free software. However, the C version of "Link Up" has been used successfully with both B-flat and E-flat instruments, and in mixed ensembles where a range of transposing and non-transposing instruments were working together.

## Equipment needed for the sessions

The most important piece of equipment, apart from the instruments themselves, is a high-quality means of playing the audio tracks. It is important that the playback sound is powerful enough for the track to be heard even when all the students are playing together.

## Which students can take part?

All students can take part. Each learner will find her own route through the task, at her own level.

## Teacher preparation

Because of the many demands that will be made upon you, it is best if you know how to play at least some of the tracks fairly confidently by ear before starting.

## Notions of "correctness" and "incorrectness," "wrong" and "right"

I use the terms "correctness," "incorrectness," "wrong," and "right" throughout this handbook advisedly. What might be considered "wrong" in a notational context might, in the context of the approaches taken here, be considered adequate, or as a creative, improvisatory embellishment which is to be encouraged. The reasons for this are complex and how a judgement is made will depend on the teacher, the task in hand and the needs of individual learners.

Photo © David Baker
as part of the Ear
Playing Project,
http://earplaying
.ioe.ac.uk

# 10

# HeLP in ensemble settings: the basic steps

• At the start of the first session, after having tuned up, explain to the ensemble that they are going to learn a piece of music by ear. Then, listen together to one of the full tracks, chosen from the popular-styles section of the audio materials. Then ask the students to get their instruments ready and explain they will now hear the bass part on its own. *Whilst the track is playing,* ask them to try to find the notes and to play along. You may wish to start with one section of the ensemble first whilst the others listen; then ask another section to have a go whilst the first section continues to play; or you may prefer to let everyone try together.

• Once most of the students have got the basic notes of the line, not necessarily all correct but in such a way that they are playing together with some continuity, this can be considered adequate basis from which to move on. It would be a mistake to insist on absolute correctness, although you will undoubtedly wish to give guidance. The point of this exercise is to free up the learners and make them reliant on their ears and their improvisatory potential.

• Once the bass line has been learnt in this way, move on to the next track and repeat the process. Once two or three tracks have been learnt, there are many activities or games as described below, that can be played using the different parts. These games can make the activity fun and give the students the opportunity to get into the flow of the music.

You may wish to do these activities with just the bass line playing on the audio, or you may quickly find that the students no longer need that support but can keep going without it. Having a drummer or any player with good rhythmic sense on a loud instrument will help, and you yourself can play that role. Games can include:

• Having different ensemble sections play one riff, whilst another section plays a different riff, and so on.

• Having different sections play at different times but allowing each individual player to decide which riff to play.

• Allowing anyone to swap riffs at any time.

- Playing "throw and catch": one player fixes on another player and tries to throw them the riff that they are playing; the other player tries to catch it; they swap riffs, ideally, whilst keeping the flow.

- Assigning a point when everyone swaps to a different riff.

- Assigning a point when each section swaps to a different riff.

- Using hand-signs to switch riffs.

- Passing riffs around the ensemble.

- Varying the riffs by the use of different techniques such as pizzicato.

- Adding other parts or percussion.

- Introducing repeats at various points, or a *da capo*.

- Encouraging able ensemble members to take a solo and improvise over the riffs.

- Appointing a student to be a musical leader.

- Telling each player to decide when to drop out, until there is only player left, who should close the piece carefully.

- Organising an ending by, for example, everyone playing a chord note three times with rests in between.

Photo © David Baker
as part of the Ear
Playing Project,
http://earplaying
.ioe.ac.uk

# 11

# How are students likely to respond?

In the original research with instrumental tuition, I noticed four main ways in which students seemed to be approaching the task. When faced with a larger ensemble, it is harder to identify and distinguish the approaches of different individuals because there are so many more students, and also because the students are likely to be watching and copying each other from the outset, as well as listening. Nonetheless, interestingly, from our observations and the comments of teachers, there are likely to be signs of the same or similar learning styles.

## Learning styles

1. The "impulsive learning style" in the ensemble setting

   In any given ensemble of say, twenty-five, you may notice a small handful of students who appear confident and who set about finding notes fairly unhesitatingly. Some of them will quickly play correct notes, but many will play an approximation of the music, often well in time but with the wrong pitches. Amongst these students, some will continue to play this incorrect version without any apparent concern and without showing any signs of listening to the recording or to the other students in order to check what they are playing. In the initial stages, it is important that you allow them to get into the flow of the music and do not stop them to correct them immediately. You can gently lead them to more accuracy as the sessions go on, if you deem it appropriate.

2. The "practical learning style" in the ensemble setting

   Some students may appear to be listening carefully to the track and/or to other students in the ensemble who they think are getting the notes right. They may seek the correct notes by quietly playing up or down a scale until they hit upon a note that sounds right. They are likely to recognise a correct note and then use it as an anchor from which to find other notes.

3. The "shot-in-the-dark learning style" in the ensemble setting

   Some students are likely to appear completely thrown by the task and very hesitant to play a note at all. Even when they do play, they may appear to be arbitrarily selecting any note that comes into their heads, without seeming to connect it to the task. Often such students are anxious and do not wish to be seen making what they think is a mistake. In such cases, your guidance will be needed at an earlier stage than with other students. In many cases, though, this does not mean that they do not want to do the task; it is quite surprising that students who exhibit such an approach are often ones who express a high level of enjoyment later on.

4. The "theoretical learning style" in the ensemble setting

Some students will ask questions or make comments such as "Which notes am I going to play?" or "I don't understand this—what are we supposed to be doing?" It is best to simply reiterate that the task is to listen and copy the music by ear. These students will see that others in the ensemble have different ideas about how to approach the task and will begin to join in.

## Pitch and rhythm in the ensemble setting

You may be taken a little by surprise by witnessing a small number of students who appear to display so-called perfect pitch or absolute pitch. They will go straight to the correct starting note and, in some cases, other consecutive notes as well. Other students will display excellent rhythmic sense and be able to play accurately in time with the recording, but not necessarily evidencing a correspondingly good pitch sense.

*Ensemble teacher:* The girl [age eight] on the glockenspiel—did you hear her? *She* found the right notes! It's almost suspicious; it's almost like I told them last week what we were going to do! I promise you I didn't! I don't know how they do it; it's quite bizarre, I find it quite bizarre.

*Ensemble teacher:* There's a boy that's coming today and he's never had a piano lesson in his life, and he plays the keyboard; and I don't know how he does it, but he just seems to know what to do. I said to him "Have you got a keyboard at home?" and he said "No." So how does he know what to do?

## Other possible learning styles

As with all aspects of this discussion, you may notice other learning styles than those already mentioned. Also, some learners may have been spontaneously applying previous knowledge, either from music theory or from pieces they had already played.

## From learning style to learning strategy in the ensemble setting

Although some students will begin by exhibiting some of the learning styles described earlier, all of them will of course develop as time goes by. Many who start off by taking "shots in the dark," for example, will gradually become more attuned to the task and thus develop strategies by which to help themselves. These could include using an anchor note from which to seek other notes, listening more carefully, or playing up and down scalar patterns to find notes. This will occur as they listen and watch others in the ensemble, and as they respond to your input.

51

52

# 12

# Teaching strategies: the role of the teacher in HeLP ensemble settings

The role of the teacher in ensemble settings includes leading the session by being in control of the ensemble and the recording; encouraging, guiding, modelling, giving hints about what the notes are; and most importantly, using your professional judgement as to what point it is best to actually tell a note name or show the position of a note on an instrument. The more students are involved at any one time, the more direction from the teacher is required in order to coordinate activities and keep everyone involved.

Here follows a slightly edited transcript of an ensemble session, which took part in our research, involving an extracurricular rehearsal in a primary school. The session was led by a specialist music teacher who coordinated music in the school for two days a week. The ensemble was made up of twenty-five children aged seven to eleven, playing a range of instruments. This was the third rehearsal of the term and was their first rehearsal of this piece. In the previous term the teacher had done "Link Up" (from the HeLP strategies) with thirteen of the children—that session is the one that was photographed for this part of the book. Since that time, more children had joined the group. Six of the children had never played in a band before, and many did not take individual instrumental lessons; most of these joined in on percussion, keyboards, ukuleles, and recorders. Some of the students had never played these instruments until three weeks before, and most had less than a year's experience.

In order to accommodate such varied needs, the teacher had developed her own materials, using the HeLP strategies of listening to a repeated riff or melody and playing it by ear. However, rather than everyone learning the same melody at the same time, she had written different melodies for different sections. In the transcript example, many of the teaching strategies mentioned earlier—encouraging, guiding, giving hints, and telling note names—are discernable.

### EX. 3: USING HELP WITH A MIXED ENSEMBLE IN A SCHOOL LUNCH PERIOD, WITH CHILDREN AGED SEVEN TO TEN.

(The teacher turns the piece on and they listen to the whole, then they all listen to the violin part.)

*Teacher:* Are you ready, violins?

(The part is: minim (half note) G, minim (half note) G, semibreve (whole note) D, repeated four times, with a percussion backing. She plays it on the keyboard to make it louder. No one plays anything.)

*Teacher:* Try a note and see what you can get! That's the lower one, would it help if I tell you that? That lower one is on the low string. (It carries on.) This one's G.

(Some students start joining in from the G, and then getting the D by themselves. Several students get it hesitatingly. The procedure is then repeated with the two flutes. The teacher has written a separate part for them, and the notes are E–E–E–E all crotchets (quarter notes), then D semibreve (whole note). The rest of the band wait patiently but the teacher did say afterwards she doesn't usually make students wait for so long between playing. The flutes start to get the notes.)

*Teacher:* What can you hear on the fifth one—does it go lower or higher?

(One student has the correct starting note, then goes too low; then they both get it right. The teacher then puts the violins and flutes together. Some students have it correctly, they all just keep playing and playing it round and round; they are all getting the pitches with some students a bit wobbly on the rhythm, but basically all there. She then repeats the procedure with the other instrumental sections. The recorders join in with the flute part, almost straightr away, then clarinets, which have a new part—G minim (half note), G minim (half note), A semibreve (whole note)—and they get it almost straight away. Then these instruments all play together. Then she adds the ukuleles, the players of which already know how to play three chords.)

*Teacher:* Ukuleles, you're going to need a chord to fit in with that. So everybody else play, and ukuleles, see if you can find a chord which fits in with that.

(They try; she encourages and goes around the class whilst the others play and repeat the phrase nonstop; she shows some of them where notes are on their instruments, others seem to have found the notes by themselves.)

*Teacher:* Well done, listen!

(She continues to encourage and guide but without giving away note names directly. Then she adds the saxes. She plays and holds down a note on the keyboard. One of the saxes gets it immediately, then moves straight on to the next note without being told. Then she adds bass guitar. Lots of the children ask to go off to the toilet at this point, which she allows them to do. A boy, Danny, has been fiddling with his euphonium throughout this process and has not yet played a note.)

*Teacher:* Are you alright, Danny?

*Danny:* Yeah, it's just making a funny noise.

(Various organisational things are going on. Then the teacher asks the pianos, of which there are two in the room, to join in.)

*Teacher:* Keep listening—see if you can fit in with the song.

(They all play together. It's a racket, but you can just about make out the correct pitches. She puts the recording of the full track back on for a few bars, then they start up again and it's better; the saxes, however, are not changing note; this is probably because she didn't spot that problem earlier.)

*Teacher:* Let's hear pianos and keyboards; are you listening pianos and keyboards?

(She puts the recording back on, of just their parts, which are slightly different from the others. They play D–C–B crotchets (quarter notes) whilst the other parts are holding their semibreve (whole note).)

*Student:* I don't know this song.

*Teacher:* No, you've never heard it 'cause I made it up!

(She has to put the recording back on. After a few bars of listening, a boy on the keyboard goes straight to the first notes correctly, but he is not apparently hearing the next bit. I gave him a little help, but he didn't need it as he seemed incredibly confident that he knew what the notes were and had no fear of the task. Some others are getting them high up; it is all coming together. The glocks are joining in. She then adds in percussion.)

*Teacher:* Are you listening percussion? What can you hear?

(The percussion part on the recording is playing. A girl on drum-kit (who is taking drum lessons) is playing a basic rock beat; others join in with whatever, not particularly related to the recording. They all listen quietly. The teacher adds bass guitar with the same procedure. It has G minim (half note)–G minim (half note)–up to D crotchet (quarter note)–E crotchet (quarter note)–D minim (half note); the player listens and tries to find notes, eventually alighting on some that are about right. Several children arrive back from the toilet and settle down.)

*Teacher:* Danny, I've not actually heard you play yet.

(Then they try as a whole ensemble to play the whole thing (i.e., eight bars of two repeated bars four times). She counts them in. They come in well. After the first two bars, Danny, who has had only four lessons on his euphonium, finally picks up the instrument and puts it to his lips for the first time. He plays a note— and it is the correct starting note! They all play the riffs four times and that's it. Everyone seems to be enjoying it!)

Teachers can usefully model by playing instruments themselves so that students can learn by watching as well as listening. In settings where everyone is playing the same or a similar instrument, such as a string orchestra, the teacher is likely to do more playing and directing. In settings where a number of very different instruments are being played, and particularly those where there is a range of ability levels, a correspondingly wide range of approaches are needed. Ideally, teachers should be able to seek and correctly find pitches, even at a basic level on as many of the instruments as possible.

55

Building on and adding to the example above, useful teaching strategies in ensemble settings can include:

- Modelling by playing one's own instrument(s).

- Modelling by taking an instrument being played by a student and showing them some of the notes.

- Giving hints about what the notes are and how to find them, but without giving actual note names.

- Giving actual note names, particularly the name of the starting note, then allowing students to try to find the next notes themselves.

- Encouraging students to try out notes without fear of being told they are wrong.

- Encouraging students to listen to the recording and to listen to themselves and each other.

- Asking questions about the music and guiding students' knowledge about its structure.

- Connecting the music to theory, if appropriate, such as notions of key, scale, chord, or musical form.

It is best to avoid picking out the names of individual students, whether it is to praise them, help them, or criticise them, as this is likely to make them self-conscious and may lead to a loss of confidence or concentration. It is also best to avoid bringing in technical terms or theory too soon. Being asked to play by ear is enough without being overloaded with factual information at the same time. There are other times for theory, which will come in useful later, once the ensemble has developed some confidence with the piece. Stick to encouragement as much as possible and to helping the students find the pitches and rhythms.

As well as, or instead of, using the strategies in the ways described above, mixed ensembles can quite easily be put together within a school, by combining aural work initially done in instrumental tuition. For example, students taking flute, violin, and brass lessons can all learn one or more of the riffs or pieces by ear in their instrumental lesson, then come together for a mixed-ensemble workshop or performance.

Photo © David Baker
as part of the Ear
Playing Project,
http://earplaying
.ioe.ac.uk

# 13

# What were the overall views of the participants?

The teachers who participated in the ensemble strategies were all also involved in the instrumental strategies, so their views are subsumed largely in part 1 of this book. With specific reference to how the strategies worked with ensembles the teachers were extremely enthusiastic. They reported being surprised at how successful this was, particularly in terms of increasing students' confidence and introducing an activity the students seemed to find very enjoyable. They also found it interesting to watch their students learning by ear in ensembles. In many cases teachers were astonished that some students were able to pick out correct pitches without help, which was something they had not previously expected to find. They also felt that the students benefitted from developing their skills in ear-playing, ensemble-playing, and listening to themselves and each other in particularly close ways.

As well as with children and young people, we used the strategies in thirteen teacher-induction sessions, involving more than two hundred and fifty teachers in mixed ensembles of between ten to forty-five teachers, many of whom were playing their second or third instrument. Participants found it fun and described it as an ear-opening as well as eye-opening experience to try out the strategies themselves in this manner, and to witness the different approaches taken by their peers.

59

# PART 3

# HeLP in classroom settings

Photo © Emile Holba,
www.emileholba
.co.uk, courtesy of
Musical Futures,
www.musicalfutures
.org

# Introduction

## The aims of HeLP in classroom settings are:

- To enhance students' motivation and enjoyment.

- To show students some basic steps involved in ear-playing, which they may not otherwise come across, based on popular musicians' informal learning practices.

- To engage with students' musical tastes and use their own music in the classroom in a way that stretches their knowledge, understanding, and skill.

- To increase students' critical listening and appreciation skills.

- To increase students' pitch sense and rhythmic sense.

- To increase students' ability to play together in a small group without the necessity of a permanently present teacher as musical leader.

- To increase group cooperation.

- To enable students to exercise and develop leadership skills.

- To enable students to develop learner autonomy.

- To include students of all abilities in the same task.

- To show students that their musical taste, judgement, and innate musical skill are respected and recognised within the classroom.

- To give teachers a route into introducing informal learning practices, supported by suggestions for how to incorporate these into the formal setting of the classroom.

- To give teachers insights into aspects of their students' musicality, potential, and personalities, of which they may have previously been unaware.

## Who participated in the classroom research and on which instruments?

The research phase of HeLP in classroom settings has a history going back to 2002, when I first tried the strategies in a generalist classroom of thirteen- to fourteen-year-olds in a central London school. Two years later, funded by the Esmée Fairbairn Foundation, I repeated and extended the work in three other schools in London, again working with students aged thirteen to fourteen. During that time I was invited to work with Hertfordshire Music Service in order to create what became known as the "informal learning" pathway, in a major national project in the UK, Musical Futures (www.musicalfutures. org). This involved using the strategies and conducting research in four other secondary schools during the academic year 2004–5, then another thirteen schools the following year. Since that time, thanks to the continued support of Musical Futures by the Paul Hamlyn Foundation, and the expert and dedicated work of the Musical Futures team and their Champion Schools, the strategies have been taken up by thousands of schools both in the UK and other countries. At this time, Musical Futures itself is running in Australia and Canada, and the informal learning model is being or has been incorporated in various research and classroom-teaching settings in Singapore, the United States, Uganda, Brazil, Bali, Thailand, and other countries.

The approach was originally designed for students aged thirteen to fourteen, but in many places, particularly Australia, it has been used successfully with children aged ten or under. In addition, the strategies have been used in numerous induction days for classroom teachers, organised and delivered by Musical Futures, and also thirteen training days for instrumental teachers as part of the Ear Playing Project in the UK, Brazil, Argentina and Singapore. Appendices A and C give lists of some of the main publications and websites relating specifically to the informal learning work which took place before and during Musical Futures.

The success of the classroom project depends on, amongst other things, having enough instruments for each student, mainly pitched instruments, with some percussion for each group; enough space for classes to break out into small groups, which will not overly disturb each other; and enough audio-playback equipment for each small group to hear their music. In places where instruments, space, and playback equipment are scarce, any interested teachers may wish to try the project on a small-scale basis, possibly as an extracurricular activity.

65

Photo © Emile Holba,
www.emileholba
.co.uk, courtesy of
Musical Futures,
www.musicalfutures
.org

# 15

# HeLP in classroom settings: preliminary practicalities

## Audio materials

For an explanation of what is contained in the audio materials please refer to Note on the Text: "The audio-materials: an overview" (xx) and appendix E, which contains a complete track listing. This is also shown on the handbook's website.

For HeLP in the classroom setting, the website's popular styles are primarily recommended, but they are used in stage 2 rather than stage 1. Once you are familiar with the strategies and the nature of the audio materials, teachers may wish to create their own specially tailored materials. You can alternatively slow down the given tracks, or change their keys using a range of freely available software, if you wish to do so. The main characteristic of the materials, which is important to replicate, is that each part should involve a riff of two to four bars and should be played continuously for around two minutes. This gives the students enough time to hear what is going on, try out notes, use notes as anchors, and keep on trying. It is probably best to try out the given materials yourself first so as to fully understand how they function.

It is not necessarily recommended that you use the classical pieces in generalist classrooms, partly (but by no means entirely) because the students are liable to say they do not like this kind of music; and partly (but again not entirely) because the classical pieces are generally more difficult to learn, since they tend to contain longer-breathed phrasing, and less internal repetition. Having said that, we used them in four schools as part of the research, with largely successful and rather interesting results; and several other schools have used them since.

## The time frame

HeLP in the classroom is organised in three stages. However, as with instrumental tuition, teachers may wish to make their own combinations and ordering of stages. Please see the flowcharts of possible options in section 17. For the purposes of the discussion here I have focused on the main recommended combination, as in Option A.

The first stage involves free choice. The reason for suggesting that this goes first is partly that it is the most realistic way to adapt the informal learning practices of young popular musicians—and the motivation, enjoyment and skill-development that are associated with them—into the classroom environment. It drops students straight into the so-called deep end of the metaphorical swimming pool, where they quickly learn to swim;

it opens their ears to music in a way that most of them have not previously experienced (unless you have done similar aural copying work with them); and it is likely to immediately increase motivation and willingness to be involved. Free choice is recommended as the first stage, regardless of how much or how little group performance work the students have done before; regardless of how familiar they are with how to play the instruments they have chosen; and regardless of how much skill and knowledge you and others have already provided them with.

The recommended stage 2 involves a choice from the popular-style pieces on the handbook's website. This is more teacher-directed, in two ways. First, it involves a piece of music provided by the teacher, and which is bound to be easier and more approachable than anything the students are likely to have chosen for themselves. Second, as well as the full piece, the website gives the individual tracks independently, with each riff being repeated on its own for around two minutes.

When this stage is introduced, because it uses music that the students have not chosen for themselves, their motivation may dip a little. Overall, though, motivation will probably return quickly and remain high. This is because during stage 1 the students will have already understood something profound about the way music is put together and how musical skills can be acquired, using their own chosen styles. In addition, coming after the freedom of stage 1, the greater structure of stage 2 is beneficial in that performance and listening skills, as well as the group cooperation skills acquired in stage 1, can be further developed.

The third stage again involves free choice and is in that sense a repetition of stage 1. However, some interesting new developments in students' approaches might be discernible when they have this second chance to choose their own music (see section 18). Following this, teachers may wish to revisit the audio materials and repeat stage 2 at some point, create their own materials, or use the website's classical materials.

Some teachers might feel nervous about allowing free choice as the first step and thus may prefer to start with the popular pieces from the website. Or they might wish to use their own choice of music with the tracks broken down in the same way, and only then move on to the students' free choice. Others may prefer to do only one of the stages. It may be worth trying various ways to see which suits you and your school best.

Each stage takes place in normal curriculum time, which in many schools is about an hour once a week. Alternatively, the stages can take place as an extracurricular activity. Either way, a fifty-minute lesson is just about long enough; but a ninety-minute lesson is ideal. Each stage takes place over a period of three to six lessons. However, the exact length of each stage is up to teachers' judgement and preferences, and will vary from school to school.

## Aims, objectives, learning outcomes, lesson structure or other requirements

If working in a context where you are required to formally identify learning outcomes, aims and objectives, lesson structure, and so on, it is possible to do this by breaking down the activities into their component parts, designating them with an appropriate label, observing what students are doing, and identifying it as a learning outcome. Ideally the structure of each lesson is relatively free, and in some lessons students can spend the entire time working in small groups. In this sense, it is not necessary to have separate targets and objectives for every lesson. Rather, the overall aim of listening to a song and copying it is an ongoing objective that stretches over a number of lessons.

## Which instruments can be used?

It is important that each student has an instrument to play, (unless they choose to use their voice for some or all of the time), and that the majority of the instruments are pitched. Orff instruments can be used successfully, as can any combination of keyboards, guitars or other plucked strings, recorders or other classroom instruments, as well as untuned percussion and homemade instruments. If it is possible to use rock instruments—electric guitars, electric bass guitars, and drum-kits—this is ideal, but it is not essential. Students should also be encouraged to bring in their own instruments, whether these are orchestral or popular music instruments, home-made or whatever. We found many of those who played orchestral instruments, particularly ones that are strongly associated with classical music, refrained from bringing them in at first, except when we were using the classical tracks; but in time these students are likely to become more willing to use them with popular styles as well.

Some students are likely to choose to use their voices, particularly in singing both the lead and any backing vocals that are in their song. The voice can also be used to render instrumental parts, especially in schools where there is a scarcity of instruments. This approach, using nothing but voices to replicate the instrumental track "Dreaming" (on the handbook's website) has been tried successfully in a pilot study in Uganda.

The project can alternatively be carried out in a keyboard laboratory or by using computers where students are working in twos and threes with headphones. In this handbook the guidance is for use with instruments in small groups, but teachers will be able to adapt the approach for computers, keyboard labs or other contexts if desired.

## Equipment needed for the lessons

As well as the instruments as discussed above, the main equipment needed is sufficient means of audio playback so that each small group can listen to the music they are copying. This could be in the form of CD players, computers, iPods, or other equipment. The quality of the audio playback need not be excellent, but it does need to have sufficient volume so that it can be heard over the students' instruments.

In stages 1 and 3, students are asked to bring their own music to the lessons. They may use various different electronic means to do this, such as iPods. It may be necessary to clear permission for some playback devices to be brought into the school, depending on school policy. The use of CDs can be helpful here, and it is particularly helpful if teachers can make copies of the students' chosen music, once it has been decided upon. Either way, a means of amplifying the music, such as iPod or MP3 speakers, a computer, or a CD player, is needed for each small group.

In stage 2, students copy music from the popular-style audio materials on the HeLP website. The teacher will need to provide an audio recording of the tracks for each small group, and a way for them to play back the recording.

## Space

Space is usually the most difficult requirement for HeLP in a school. The students split up into small groups of normally three to six, and therefore enough spaces are needed for them to work without too much noise disturbance from neighbouring groups. Teachers need to be within easy reach of every group, so placing them in disparate rooms all around the school is an unlikely option in most cases (spaces that were used in our research schools often included corridors, stockrooms or nearby spare classrooms). Where it is impossible for teachers to find such spaces during normal school hours, HeLP can be done as an extracurricular activity, at times when more rooms are available. Good sound-proofing is not essential, but there must be some physical separation between spaces so that students within each group can hear themselves, each other, and most particularly, the recording they are copying.

## Which students can take part?

HeLP in the classroom is designed for all students, including those who take specialist instrumental lessons and those who have never played before. HeLP can be employed in generalist mixed ability or specialist elective classes, and it can work with students aged from ten upwards, or younger if adapted; but the approach described in this handbook is particularly suitable for ages thirteen to sixteen

Differentiation is by outcome: rather than the teacher giving a different task to each student depending on the student's ability, all the students undertake the same task, and each individual approaches the task at their own level.

## Size of the small groups

It is possible for a student to work alone, or for a group of up to seven or eight students to work together. The ideal group size is four to five.

## Teacher preparation

If you have a popular, jazz, or folk music background, or other ear-playing experience, it will be relatively straightforward to help students find pitches. Even for experienced ear-players, though, the general noise and bustle of the environment can make this challenging. If you are a classical player who has only played from notation, it may be helpful to practice some ear-playing in advance of the first lesson. This can be done using some of the materials on the handbook's website if desired.

The teacher should also be familiar with the range of instruments available to the students in order to be able to help them find pitches and to model performance techniques. However, teachers do not need advanced skills on all the instruments.

## Communications within the school

In schools where noisy small-group work is not customary, it is a good idea to speak to senior members of staff, and other staff whose teaching rooms might be close by, to make sure they are forewarned about possible disturbances. If there are significant doubts about the value of the activity, colleagues can perhaps be referred to the extensive research in appendices A and B, and the websites in appendix C.

## Notions of "correctness" and "incorrectness," "wrong," and "right"

I use the terms "correctness," "incorrectness," "wrong," and "right" throughout this handbook advisedly. What might be considered "wrong" in a notational context might, in the context of the approaches taken here, be considered adequate, or as a creative, improvisatory embellishment, which is to be encouraged. The reasons for this are complex and how a judgement is made will depend on the teacher, the task in hand and the needs of individual learners.

Photo © Emile Holba,
www.emileholba
.co.uk, courtesy of
Musical Futures,
www.musicalfutures
.org

# 16

# HeLP in classroom settings: the basic steps

## Stage 1: Free choice: "Into the deep end": introducing informal learning into the classroom

In this initial stage students are "dropped into the deep end," emulating as nearly as possible the real-life learning practices of young, beginner popular musicians. Here, lesson 1 is outlined in detail, followed by suggestions for how to implement the stage overall.

Students are asked to bring in their own music for the first lesson. It is most likely they will bring pop songs, although if anyone asks whether they can bring any other kind of music, the answer is "of course—yes!" Students should feel able to bring in music from any style, including electronically generated music, music that is largely made of unpitched rhythms, rapped rather than sung words, and the like. This part of the method is about students' choice and identity, and it is important at this early stage that teachers do not impose their opinions on the choice of music.

The only type of music that will be deemed unsuitable is that with sexist, racist, violent, or other unethical lyrics or connotations. Decisions on this will depend on school policy and on teachers' judgement. We have found students are usually very excited to bring in and copy their own music, especially if they have never been given the opportunity to do so before. They themselves know well what is likely to be considered acceptable and what is not, and most of them do not need this spelling out to them.

The stage begins with a brief class discussion of the question: "How do you think popular musicians—for example, the ones you listen to in your spare time—learn to play their instruments? How do they learn to sing, improvise, and compose music?"

While students may suggest all sorts of ideas, many of which will be correct, to date there is evidence that young people under the age of sixteen or so, generally are not clear about how music can be learnt by listening to a recording; many of them have only a vague awareness of this practice, and the majority have never tried it themselves. By doing this activity even for a few lessons, we are opening a new door of learning and opportunity to them.

Teachers should make sure that the following points are covered and profiled by the end of the discussion:

- Popular musicians may learn by taking lessons, practicing, using computers, and in other ways that students might suggest.

- They also learn by listening to recordings of their own favourite music and copying it.

- They do this by themselves and with friends; often without any teacher at all.

- They also make up their own versions of the music, alone and in groups.

- They also improvise and compose their own music.

Students may suggest that musicians use computers to make their own music, take lessons, learn from the Internet, learn from teachers, or learn from books. These are valid answers, but students should be alerted to the fact that those individuals who use these approaches still spend time listening to and familiarising themselves with other musicians' work, as part of their own creative processes.

Teachers then explain that for the next few lessons, students are going to learn informally, as far as possible, by:

- Working in small friendship groups.

- Choosing any piece they wish from among their own music (barring unsuitable lyrics and connotations).

- Choosing instruments, according to availability in the school.

- Listening to and copying the music in whatever ways they wish.

It should also be explained that:

- Teachers will *initially* stand back and observe what students are doing. This means teachers will not intervene to suggest that certain music is too difficult or too easy, or that particular instruments are too hard to play or will not sound good together, and so on.

- Then the teacher will try to take on students' perspectives and thus come to an understanding of the goals that students are setting for themselves.

- At around the third lesson, teachers will start to offer a range of guidance, suggestions and explanations, and will model how to seek pitches and how to play instruments.

At this point it is important to establish ground rules concerning the norms of behaviour expected by the individual teacher, the department, and the school.

## Getting started with the task itself

- Students get into small friendship groups. We have found it unlikely that individuals are left out, but if this happens it is only your professional judgement that can decide whether a group should be requested to include a particular student, or whether that student would benefit by working on their own.

- The groups take their audio equipment and a range of their own music into a practice space and choose one song (they nearly always choose songs rather than instrumental pieces when they first do this task, so I refer to "songs" rather than "pieces"). At this first stage, the students will be more interested in selecting songs that they like, rather than ones that they think will be easy or suitable to copy. It is essential that they are allowed to choose, and that they enjoy and identify with the music they are working on. Therefore no advice from teachers is required about the choice of song, unless it is explicitly requested by students or unless the teacher feels help is needed to get the group going (see section 19).

- Choosing the song may take the remainder of the first lesson, plus some or all the next lesson. What if the group fails to settle on a song after two lessons? The best thing here is to remind them that unless they choose one soon, they will not be able to get anything done. In most cases, motivation is high enough for them to decide to make compromises. You may at this point wish to suggest something that you think is suitable, although it is best to leave the choice entirely to the students if agreement can be reached that way.

- Students then select instruments to play and begin the task. If possible teachers should encourage any students who have their own instruments to bring them to the lessons.

Once students have chosen their song, it is helpful if each group, or the teacher, makes a copy of it during or after the lesson for safekeeping, in case the recording is not available in subsequent weeks. In addition, having some spare recordings of recent hits is a good standby in case students forget their own music; this option, however, will never make a fully satisfactory substitution for their own choice.

## Continuing with the task

The task then continues for two to four or five additional lessons, depending on the teacher's judgement and preference. At the beginning of each lesson students may need little or no reminding about the nature of the task; they are more likely to be frustrated by long plenary sessions, as in the student commentary: "Can't we just come in and get on with it? We know exactly what we need to do, we don't need reminding of it!" In one school where the approach was particularly successful, with only a fifty-minute lesson, the teacher allowed students to go straight to their practice rooms without any plenary, and went around marking the register while they were settling down. Plenary sessions then took place as and when the task called for them.

It is good if some lessons can end with group performances. Peer-assessment, listening to, and watching each other are central parts of informal learning practices, and can lead to some useful exchange of musical ideas and knowledge between students. They are usually fascinated to hear and see their peers performing their musical products, and this can lead to some careful listening too. Some teachers might like to make audio recordings or videos of the performances. Some of the performances can be refined and included in the larger context of a school concert.

## Stage 2: Popular styles with short riffs in separate parts for the classroom

Having been dropped into the deep end in stage 1, students are now given more guidance and structure through a broken-down "musical model" of a song using the popular-style audio materials on the handbook's website or other music of your choice, arranged in such a way as to involve repeated riffs on separate tracks.

## Teacher-directed, interim lessons

Some teachers might like to place one or more formal lessons between the HeLP stages 1 and 2, or at some other point. This can involve demonstrating and practicing instrumental skills on a range of instruments, rehearsing aspects of ensemble playing and keeping time, or other more theoretical aspects such as learning about note-names, scales, chords, modes, or keys.

It can also be useful to use a "carousel" system by dividing up the class into instrumental groups rather than friendship groups. For example, five students can all work on the same instrument to learn the same riff together; then the groups can all move around so that each group learns a different riff on a different instrument. Mixed groups can then be put together for performances. All this of course depends on the age and experience of the learners and the judgement of the teacher.

## The stage 2 task itself

For stage 2 of the project, with or without the aforementioned additional lesson or lessons, recommended steps are:

- Explain that students will still be copying music from a recording, but this time they will be given the music, broken down into separate parts to make it easier to hear and copy them.

- Play the class an extract of one or both of the audio materials on the HeLP website, "Dreaming" or "Link Up." You may wish to choose one of these and reserve the other one for another time; or you may wish to suggest that each small group can decide between the two.

- Explain that separate parts on the recording tend to go from easy to more difficult.

- Play a selection of the separate tracks.

- Demonstrate how to play different tracks, that is parts, on a suitable instrument.

- Show how the parts can be combined together. This can be done by asking one or two of the more able students to demonstrate different parts to the rest of the class, or by doing it yourself. Playing the bass line or some other part on the audio recording whilst you or one or more students play a different line is also helpful.

- Play along with those students or the recording in such as way as to model how the riffs can be switched around and combined within a band.

Through such activities, explain and demonstrate to students that:

- The task is to copy and play along with the track on their chosen instruments.

- It is best to start with the easy parts first, that is, by using tracks in the numbered order, and not all tracks need to be learnt.

- Riffs can be played any number of times, in any order and any combination.

- Students can play with or without the audio recording.

- Each group should aim to make up its own version of the music by putting the parts together, and may add new riffs if desired.

- Split into small groups, each with a means of playing the recordings and a selection of instruments, then go into separate spaces and begin.

Continuation lessons may range in number from three to five, and as with stage 1, it is good if there are some group performances either during or at the end of the process.

## Stage 3: The deep end revisited, and further work

Building on the experience of the deep end in stage 1, combined with the more structured guidance of the prepared audio tracks in stage 2, students can be given a second opportunity to choose their own music and work in their own ways in stage 3. This stage does not have to follow stage 2 immediately but could be placed at any point in the school year. After one or more of the stages, you may wish to move on to group composition, improvisation, and/or the use of other music. This can involve using world music, the classical tracks from the Help website, or any other materials you may wish to make.

# 17

# Some possible combinations and orders of stages the classroom context

The flowcharts shown in figures 4, 5, 6, 7, and 8 illustrate the different stages as they have been described here along with some further possible combinations.

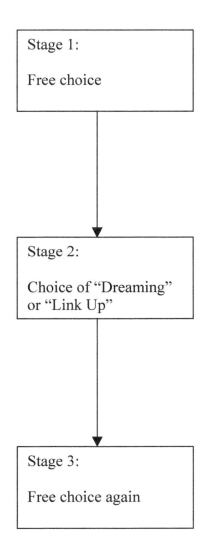

**Figure 4**
Option A: the classroom

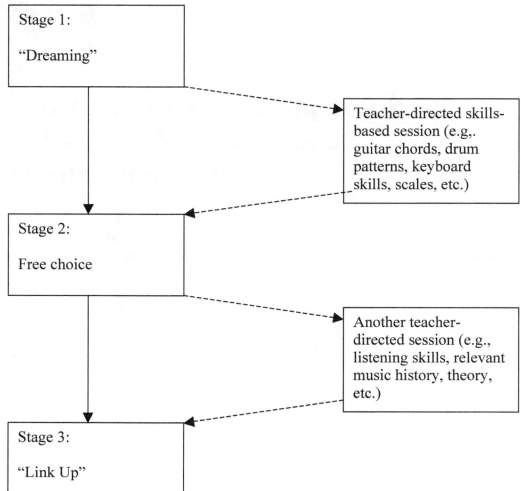

**Figure 5**
Option B: the classroom (where teachers wish to place other more teacher-directed sessions in between the stages)

Stage 1:
"Dreaming"

Teacher-directed skills-based session (e.g,. guitar chords, drum patterns, keyboard skills, scales, etc.)

Stage 2:
Free choice

Another teacher-directed session (e.g., listening skills, relevant music history, theory, etc.)

Stage 3:
"Link Up"

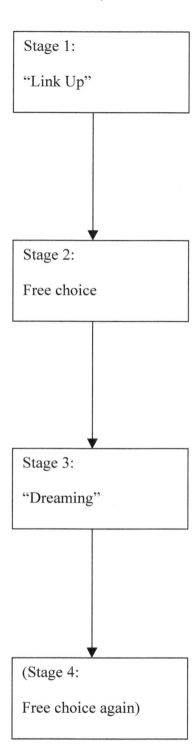

| Stage 1: |
| "Link Up" |

| Stage 2: |
| Free choice |

| Stage 3: |
| "Dreaming" |

| (Stage 4: |
| Free choice again) |

**Figure 6**
Option C: the classroom (a good option for teachers who are unconvinced about the benefits of jumping straight into the deep end)

79

**Figure 7**

Option D: the classroom (giving even more time for students to get experience of working with structured materials before jumping into the deep end with their own music)

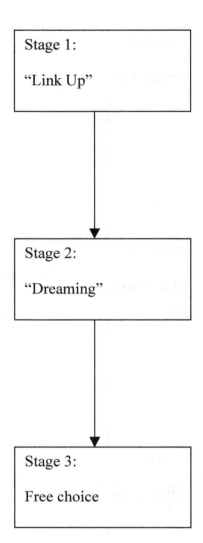

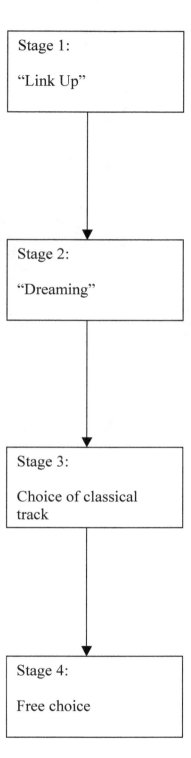

These flowcharts illustrate the potential flexibility in the choice and ordering of the different stages that can be tailored to different teachers' and students' needs in many more combinations than are given here. Many teachers will no doubt decide to simply try one stage only and take any further stages if they wish, step by step.

Photo © Emile Holba,
www.emileholba
.co.uk, courtesy of
Musical Futures,
www.musicalfutures
.org

# How are students likely to respond?

## Responses to stage 1 (free choice) in the classroom

In stage 1, when students are given free choice, they are usually highly motivated by the task. They are likely to quickly form themselves into friendship groups and will eagerly start listening to a range of music. As previously mentioned, students will almost always choose to copy a popular song, normally one currently in the charts; nonetheless, there will be national and regional differences. Choosing a song will involve discussion, negotiation, and usually some close listening. In some groups the process of settling on a song is fairly smooth and may well have been achieved by the end of the first lesson. Other groups will take two lessons. Beyond that it is advised that the teacher steps in. In some groups, inevitably, the process of selecting music is more difficult, and agreement is not reached even by the end of the third lesson. For this and other reasons too, some individuals may not settle down to the task. Arguments may break out, particularly where there are resource limitations.

These kinds of problems happen in all classrooms, and it is always up to the teacher's judgement and experience how to deal with them in fair and authoritative ways. In general, the high motivation most students feel when first introduced to this task means that so long as they are given enough space and time, enough instrumental and audio resources, and enough autonomy balanced with enough guidance (see below), the vast majority are likely to compromise their own views to select a song and, from then, stay on task.

Once a song has been chosen, the process of choosing instruments begins. Depending on availability of resources, this should be a relatively smooth process. If there is a scarcity of the most desirable instruments you will need to step in to negotiate a fair way to share.

Once both the song and the instruments have been chosen, the next thing that may happen is that one or more students in each group starts to play untuned percussion, particularly a drum-kit if it is available. Interestingly, you may notice, especially with groups who have not done this kind of activity before, that the percussionist will in some cases not play a beat or a rhythm that in any way resembles the percussion part of their chosen song, but instead will play the rhythm of the main vocal or melody line. This can happen so fleetingly and whilst so much else is going on that it may slip your attention at the time. I first noticed it when I was listening back to recordings of the lessons rather than while I was in the busy and noisy classroom environment. However, if you listen carefully for it you may indeed hear it.

What sometimes happens next is that another student who has listened to the music more accurately, or who has prior knowledge of the role of percussion, will correct the drummer. In other cases, no one in the group will appear to notice. Even in groups where this response is not noticed by the participants themselves, gradually during the course of the first one to three lessons, the students will hear more deeply inside the music, and the percussion part will start to resemble the original more closely. Many students commented following this exercise that their listening deepened, and they started to notice—in many cases for the first time—that music has "underneath parts" and is "made of layers." To some this came as a total surprise, many of whom said they had previously thought of music as containing nothing but lyrics.

Although you may be tempted to correct the drummer who is playing the rhythm of the melody at the outset, resisting that temptation for a while can lead to the students learning about the role of the percussion for themselves in a way that is more vivid and memorable than being told about it or having it demonstrated.

Another behaviour you may witness is that some groups will play together for relatively long periods of time, possibly throughout the whole recording of their chosen song and even longer. Yet, very often one, two, or all of the students may be completely out of time with each other, (and inevitably there will be lots of wrong notes as well as missing notes). Yet they are not likely to stop and correct themselves in the way that they would do if they were, say, a group of young instrumentalists playing from notation. Rather, they will often just keep on going regardless. They may phase in and out of time with each other and not appear to show signs of knowing that this is happening. Slowly, in most cases, their rhythmic sense builds and the group will start to gel. Again, guidance from you may be needed but not too much, and not too soon.

In many cases, a dip in achievement manifests itself around the third lesson. Groups who previously appeared to be playing in time together may start to play out of time; those who had previously been hitting correct pitches may seem to have forgotten what they were or how to play them; some groups who were previously cooperating may start to have disagreements. Now the teachers' sensitivity to the task, and their belief in their role, is most tightly stretched. In most cases, persistence brings reward and the achievement will start to improve, usually after a little bit of guidance from you.

Why is it common for group achievement to dip around the third lesson? One reason might be that the students start off the activity by listening hard to the recording. This keeps them playing relatively in time and together. Once they have begun to play some notes with a certain amount of success, their attention may be directed away from the recording and onto their own movements and control of the instrument. Thus they may get more out of time with the track and with each other. Similarly, at first they may confidently play rhythms, but as they listen more carefully they become focused on attempting to find correct pitches, which is generally more difficult. This seeming regression is therefore not necessarily a sign that their learning is going backwards, but may indicate that they are learning something new and more difficult.

You will probably find that the levels of group cooperation are good. In some cases this is likely to be better than usual and often better than you expected. Students generally choose for themselves and organise for each other within their groups those tasks that suit different individuals' abilities. Leaders will emerge among the students, and very often these are individuals who have not previously shown any inclination, ability, or commitment in music lessons. Students who had not previously excelled or cooperated in music classes may surprise you by showing themselves to be able and willing musicians or to possess previously hidden leadership qualities.

Additionally, as in the research with instrumental tuition and ensembles, there appeared to be four main ways in which students approached the task. With a large number of students all working in small groups in different rooms or spaces, it can be difficult to notice and assimilate the many activities and responses that are going on. The following list gives some responses you may see among individual members of groups.

## Learning styles

1. The "impulsive learning style" in the classroom setting

   Some students within their small group will start almost immediately to play an instrument, often percussion. These students may appear very confident and are likely to play loudly. This can cause difficulties for other students who are trying to speak to each other or to listen to the music. Such students are often, however, rhythmically accurate and can be useful, particularly later on, as their strong sense of beat will keep the other members of the group in time with each other. As with all students, they will respond well to encouragement and being told their skills are potentially helpful. They can, for example, be asked to devote some effort to helping other students who are less confident until such time as their own playing will be needed.

2. The "practical learning style" in the classroom setting

   Some students will be intent upon listening carefully to their chosen music. They may take a more systematic approach to seeking pitches, playing different notes, listening, and turning the audio recording on and off. As in the instrumental and ensemble settings, once a correct note has been found, they are likely to recognise it, return to it, and use it as an anchor from which to seek other notes. In some groups, where the students feel comfortable singing, one or more of them may start to sing the vocal line; sometimes one or more backing lines or harmony parts are attempted after a few lessons. One problem that such students face is the difficulty of seeking notes when there is more than one person all working together in a noisy environment. Such students can be supported by the teacher helping them find the starting pitch and then suggesting that they can seek the next pitches themselves. This is further described in the next section.

3. The "shot-in-the-dark learning style" in the classroom setting

   Some students will appear hesitant about the task. They will often stand back, watch others, and rely on learning that way rather than by experimenting with instruments. There is nothing necessarily wrong with a student learning in this way, although if you see it happening, you may think they are "doing nothing." Learning by listening and watching peers is a central informal learning practice, and it may be that for some students, this is the best way to learn.

Again, it is necessary to give them time, encouragement, and guidance, as described later.

4. The "theoretical approach" in the classroom setting

Students will inevitably ask questions, and there will be some students who ask more questions than others. Some of the questions may be related to practicalities: where to find equipment, how to assemble it, where to work, and so on; others will concern how best to organise their group; others will relate to the music and what song to choose; what the notes they are seeking are called, and how to find them on their instruments. The job of the teacher is always to answer questions, and this can be done in various ways, as described later.

## Other possible learning styles

You may notice other learning styles that we did not come across or that we noticed only amongst very small numbers of participants. For example, you might witness some learners who show signs of having perfect pitch (see parts 1 and 2); there may be students with prior experience of ear-playing who apply previous knowledge from pieces they have already played; others may use knowledge from music theory.

## Responses to Stage 2 (popular-style pieces with broken-down tracks) in the classroom

If stage 1 (free choice) is applied first, as recommended, then students are liable to complain when they are requested to use given music in stage 2. They will undoubtedly say they do not like the music, and things like "Why do we have to do this? Can't we do our own stuff?" Experience shows that once they have started on the stage 2 materials, their motivation will quickly return. The main reason is that the separate parts provided in the stage 2 audio materials make the process of copying the tracks much easier than when the students are copying their own "real-world" music, which is not divided up into separate tracks for them. Because the process in stage 2 is easier, the students' progress is faster, thus they get more immediate satisfaction. They then quickly understand what it is that they are attempting to do at a deeper level, and they also achieve a more musically successful result. This in itself feeds back to increase motivation. Teachers' and students' comments on how stage 2 (popular-style piece with separate parts) builds on stage 1 (free choice) included:

*Teacher:* They're looking at this much more in terms of structuring their work— so giving a beginning, a middle, and an end, and some groups actually thought about layering their textures and bringing in part by part. It's actually about thinking more widely about what putting together music actually entails.

*Teacher:* They put together performances in a short space of time which is a good achievement. And they all performed them with fantastic musical skills—with timing, with group work, and ensemble and listening skills.

*Student:* I think that the second stage was easiest because we had a clear place to start.

*Student:* I thought it was kind of good that we were all like at the same point, in stage 2, because before like we were all doing different songs, and some people picked a really hard song 'cause they like it, like John's group, and some people like us we picked a hard one and we weren't necessarily good enough to play it. But the song in stage 2 was good enough for everyone.

## Responses to stage 3 (free choice) in the classroom

When students are given a second chance to choose their own music, some interesting things happen. Rather than simply going for what they regard as the most popular and mainstream hits, they may begin to look and listen farther afield. Many are likely to come in to class with a wider range of musical styles to copy. One reason for this is that they now have a better awareness of the nature of the task; they have learnt about how to listen to music more carefully during their first attempt; and consequently they are more aware of what the music contains, and correspondingly, more interested in choosing music they feel will be easier for them to copy successfully. Another reason is that students are now more attuned to the way music is put together and thus are less mystified and awed by the social connotations that go along with music, such as being up to date, fashionable, and the like. When they attempt to copy their own chosen music for a second time, and particularly if this activity is preceded by stage 2 of the materials (or other materials you have prepared using similar techniques), then the students achieve more accurate and pleasing results, more quickly. Teachers' and students' comments on how stage 3 (a second opportunity for free choice), builds on stage 1 (free choice) and stage 2 (popular-style piece with separate parts) included:

*Teacher:* The accuracy I think is better this time around than it was before— they're picking it up quicker, and they're also finding it easier to put themselves right when they go wrong. They've chosen much more appropriate songs—much more riff-based stuff, and many of them have swapped around and tried different instruments and been much more confident with that as well.

*Teacher:* There was a rise in their standard definitely. They had grasped the ideas of having layers—having riffs and putting them together, putting it into a structure. They'd also got rid of the music as backing, and they were quite confident in performing it without the backing. It was recognisable just from what they were doing.

*Teacher:* What we've done with the stages has been a natural progression with the students' interests in mind—going with what they would want first. Just letting them have a go and then with a bit of guidance letting them have another go.

*Student:* It was better 'cause we knew what we were doing.

*Student:* We were like more confident and we like knew what CDs to choose— not really fast ones!

87

*Student:* You get more appreciation if you can actually play the song rather than trying to jump yourself in the deep end and choose a really hard song and you can't play it.

*Student:* The more you do it the more you're just kind of practicing the skills that you know and then you'll get even better.

Photo © Emile Holba,
www.emileholba
.co.uk, courtesy of
Musical Futures,
www.musicalfutures
.org

# 19

# Teaching strategies: the role of the teacher in HeLP classroom settings

As outlined in section 18, students are given a clear task by the teacher in the first lesson of each HeLP classroom stage. Throughout each stage, resources are organised by the teacher; ground rules, such as respect for instruments, staff, and other students, are laid down and maintained by the teacher; and in all similar respects the teacher's role is no different from what would normally be expected in any classroom. If desired, the teacher can also produce lesson plans, intended learning outcomes, aims, and objectives by breaking down the activities into component parts.

In other ways, though, the traditional relationship of teacher as all-knowing instructor, and student as unknowing apprentice, is adjusted. Students have relative freedom: they are allowed to choose who to have in their groups, within reason; to choose what music to play (in stages 1 and 3) so long as the lyrics or connotations are not unsuitable; and to select instruments for themselves from whatever the school has available. They are then given independence to approach the task and to organise themselves, set their own objectives, and steer their own course through the learning.

The teacher's role is to set the task going, then, importantly, for the first couple of lessons stand back and observe what the students are doing. During this time teachers are asked to try to understand and empathise with the goals that the students are setting for themselves. If a group is not getting down to the task at all, then the teacher will need to step in and organise them, but in general you will probably find that the majority of groups welcome the task and get down to work quickly.

Around the third lesson, students will start to need guidance of various kinds, and it is at that point that teachers step in to help them in a variety of ways to keep them at a level where they are both fulfilled, and yet challenged. Some teachers have expressed the worry that by standing back in the first few lessons, and by taking the approaches described, they will no longer be in control and thus no longer be teaching. Nothing could be farther from the truth: even during the first few lessons, standing back and observing what students are doing, noting how they are tackling the task, and attempting to understand their goals, is still part of teaching. Indeed, observation alone is an active process involving all one's attention and experience. Having stood back and observed for several lessons, the teacher is then in a position to judge what guidance is needed, when it is needed, and how to give it.

The teacher needs to have a range of musical skills and understanding in order to model on different instruments, show students how to find notes, how to hold the instrument more effectively, how to harmonise parts, and many more such skills. Teachers also find they are much in demand for technical help, such as how to set up and tune instruments.

What follows are five slightly edited transcripts from Musical Futures classrooms, and my earlier work in London schools, where the strategies were used in general, mixed-ability, non-elective music classes involving students aged thirteen to fourteen. After each example I have identified some of the teaching strategies that were in use and that can be recommended.

## EX. 4: USING HeLP IN A MIXED GENERALIST CLASSROOM

(The CD track finishes. The boy on piano, David, is showing the teacher what he's done.)

*David:* Right, it's about to start. (There is loud drumming. David demonstrates the pitches he has learnt on the piano.)

*Teacher:* That's great; do you know what the next notes are? Let's see if we can find them. Can you stop drumming for a minute and let me hear what's on the CD?

(The CD track plays. The teacher seeks pitches on the piano. Some isolated comments from the teacher and the boys. The track stops.)

*Student:* Isn't that an electric guitar?

*Teacher:* It is an electric guitar, yeah.

(The teacher shows a different boy, Lenny, how to play three notes from the song on the guitar.)

*Teacher:* Can you do it like that, do you think?

(Lots of voices and discussion all going on at the same time.)

*Teacher:* That's it, you practice doing that OK? And I'll try and play something on the piano.

*Student:* What about the drums ?

*Teacher:* I'll come back to that in a minute.

(The track starts and the boy on piano shows the teacher what he's done.)

*Teacher:* It's fantastic. It's fantastic. It's all there! That is really so good.

*Student* (to David): You got the piano sorted.

*Student:* Do we need a singer?

*Student:* What about the drums?

*Student:* Can we have the piano doing the same thing as the drums?

91

In this case, the teacher is:

- Asking a student to show her what he's done and giving encouragement.

- Requesting that students are quiet so that she can listen to the recording, then seeking pitches first on the piano, then on the guitar, and showing the students how to play them. Thus she is demonstrating the practice of listening and finding pitches by trial and error, which the students observe and can subsequently take on for themselves.

- Taking and answering questions about instruments and their roles.

### EX. 5: USING HeLP IN A MIXED GENERALIST CLASSROOM

*Teacher:* OK, in the music can you hear this? (Sings a melodic riff). Can you hear that? Why don't you try and work out what those notes are on the keyboard then.

*Student:* It's going to be up the top, isn't it?

*Student:* It's going to be low, isn't it?

(The teacher does not answer but allows the students to experiment in order to find the answer themselves. A few notes are played on the keyboard, which are approximately the right pitches.)

*Teacher:* Yep, nearly. (He sings the first note).

*Student:* Can you switch these around? (The boy on the keyboard can be heard now getting the right notes).

*Teacher:* What about finding a bit of a better sound on the keyboard, like something on the CD?

*Student:* Sir?

*Teacher:* What about the beat, Mark?

*Student:* How do you change that, (talking about the drums) 'cause that one's too loose, look how swingy it is.

*Teacher:* It should just slide out. It might need unscrewing a bit actually.

(The boy on the keyboard starts experimenting with different voices and then with the three notes of the song. A guitar is being played at same time.)

*Teacher:* That's good! Now, Andy, what would you play with him? What note is it that you play?

*Andy:* A, B, C (reading them off what someone has written with a felt pen on the keyboard).

*Teacher:* They're wrong, somebody's written completely the wrong notes on the keyboard.

*Student:* That's an A, that's a C, that's a D.

*Teacher:* Good. So what could Andy play to go with that? What notes do you need to find?

*Andy:* A, C, and D?

*Teacher:* Now see if you can find the right notes to go with him (sings the notes). OK, now start off with the A, see if you can find an A. Have a go, try one. See if it's—what did you play then?

(Andy finds the A on the keyboard).

*Teacher:* Good!

(Inaudible talk; drums are being played. The CD track is put back on and the student on the keyboard is now playing correct notes. Another student on drums is working out a beat.)

*Teacher:* OK, so you're on your own now. (He then gets them to play without the CD). Come on, together.

*Student:* Ollie, Ollie, turn the sound up!

*Teacher:* That's quite good now, come on!

*Student:* One, two, three, four (they all come in together).

*Teacher:* (Sings.) And then the tune goes over the top.

*Student:* Play it on, lads. That's quite good actually, just us three, look.

*Teacher:* Yeah, if you got some singing or vocals.

(Mark plays a drum beat again, and adds hi-hat. They play the song again with all three of them joining in. Ollie starts to play the keyboard riff up a couple of octaves as well).

In this case, the teacher is:

- Suggesting that the students listen carefully to the recording, and identifying a part of the music by singing it for them.

- Suggesting that they could work it out on the keyboard, and fielding questions about the pitch range, giving students time to work out the answer for themselves.

- Singing pitches to help a student find them.

- Suggesting the students use different sounds on the keyboard.

- Encouraging a student to be involved and to add a drum beat.

- Giving technical support with the drums.

- Asking students to identify the correct note names of the keyboard.

- Identifying the names of sounded pitches.

- Drawing back ("you're on your own now") at a point where he feels the students have got far enough to continue for a while without further help.

### EX. 6: USING HeLP IN A MIXED GENERALIST CLASSROOM

*Student:* Miss, what part of the song does that go with?

*Teacher:* It's the bass line. Let's play it again.

(The teacher puts the audio recording back on and plays along. Sandra is watching her pick out the very simple bass line. The teacher was actually showing the bass line to another girl in the group who was watching but did not show any particular response. The teacher could see Sandra showing interest so she suggested that the two girls swap roles and that Sandra comes and plays it.)

*Teacher:* Can you hear it? Can you try with this bit? (Showing some notes.)

*Sandra:* Yeah, a bit.

*Teacher:* Who wants to play it? I'll show you how to play it.

(Sandra sits at the piano, and the teacher shows her where to put her fingers. She doesn't know the names of the notes on the keyboard, or the geography of the keyboard. At first she has difficulty remembering what note she just played. The teacher gives her some ways to remember where the notes are, such as how they sit next to the black notes. In a while the teacher suggests that Sandra does not move her hand down to her lap after playing each note but keeps the fingers over the notes. She improves very quickly.)

*Teacher:* Well done! Keep it going.

(As Sandra is playing, the other girls who previously appeared to show no interest, are now craning their necks to see what she is doing and reaching for instruments themselves. The teacher shows a drum beat to another girl while Sandra continues playing the piano. They put the recording back on and Sandra gets the bass line in time almost straight away. Meanwhile the other girls are beginning to get their hand percussion together. After one more play-through they are all in time. They play right through the song once more. The singer is away today but when she comes back they will be ready for a performance.)

Here the teacher is:

- Identifying the bass line and picking it out by ear while she is being watched by a student, thus demonstrating the process of seeking pitches by trial and error.

- Noticing that one student appears more interested than another and drawing that student into the process by suggesting they swap places. Thus she gives something manageable to one member of the group, whose success at the task then attracts the attention and interest of others.

• Suggesting ways for a student to remember what she is playing.

• Showing a drum beat to another student.

## EX. 7: USING HeLP IN A MIXED GENERALIST CLASSROOM

*Teacher:* Yeah. OK, let's hear what you're up to then, lads. Try not to make a noise on your instrument until you actually mean to, because it spoils it as people aren't sure if you're meant to be playing or not. (They start playing.)

*Teacher:* OK, stop there. That sounds good. Can I suggest you start with the drummer, on his own, and then when you start doing that cha-cha-cha beat, you come in, once you've got going, and then the two guitars, because then we'll get a clearer idea of what you're up to.

*Student:* So we come in after the . . .

*Teacher:* I'll show you with my hand when to come in. Let's start with drums first. (They start.)

*Teacher:* Right, that's good. Do your duh-duh-duh a few times, and then you (to another student) come in. That was good, that was really good. You do your duh-duh-duh. That's it. Do it again then. Now you two. OK, boys. That's going to be really good.

*Student:* It's hard to do without the CD on.

*Teacher:* It sounds good without the CD on. I think you need to turn those two guitars down a bit, 'cause they're drowning everyone else out. If you can just try in the five minutes you've got left, to get that really, really crisp. Get that really crisp and do it just like you did it, first the drummer, and then he goes duh-duh-duh.

*Student:* Yeah, I'll do it about three times.

*Teacher:* Four times, four times OK? Then you, and then you two.

*Student:* And then where do we start?

*Teacher:* He does duh-duh-duh four times, then the keyboard player does it four times, then guitars.

*Student:* And then where do we stop?

*Teacher:* Well if you've got time, what you can do is one of you, maybe the keyboard player could indicate to the others when to stop by going to the others "stop" or something like that.

*Student:* STOP!

95

*Teacher:* 'Cause if you all stop together it will sound really impressive, so can you practice that in the time you've got left?

Here, the teacher is:

- Drawing the group together by requiring them to be silent and then for each player to start playing at an allotted time.

- Giving guidance about how many times to play a particular riff before other instruments come in.

- Giving hand signals to indicate when different instruments should start to play.

- Suggesting that one of the players could give the signal to stop, and other ways to organise when the players should start and stop.

- Giving encouragement, including encouraging the group to play without the audio recording in the background.

- Making suggestions about the volume balance of different instruments.

- Setting the students the task of achieving rhythmic precision over the final five minutes of the session.

## EX. 8: USING HeLP IN A MIXED GENERALIST CLASSROOM

*Teacher:* OK. Do you need any help?

*Patrick:* No.

*Teacher:* Not at all?

*Patrick:* I only know the introduction to the song, I'm the only one who can play it.

*Teacher:* Show us the introduction to the song that you do know. (Patrick plays something on guitar.)

*Teacher:* And Tom, do you know what you're meant to be doing? That you learnt last week?

*Tom:* Yeah, I wrote it down.

*Teacher:* Come on then, show me.

*Tom:* At the start, in the middle, the bit you showed me (he plays a riff on keyboard), and the other one is (plays another riff on keyboard). I don't know that bit though.

*Teacher:* Do you think we maybe need to listen to the CD and work a few more things out? Yeah?

*Student:* Yes.

*Teacher:* Can you put on the CD? Have you got a pen? (The CD track goes on. The teacher works out some chords by ear. There is a bit of messing around going on still).

*Teacher:* Ah, that's it; I think that the chorus starts there (plays note). Actually, can we play that again please, I think we've found the missing note.

(The CD comes on again. The teacher plays along on keyboard.)

*Teacher:* Now, I think the chorus goes up to there. (Some students are chatting in the background.) OK, so it goes up to there. Tom, if you listen to this, how many times can you hear this riff?

*Tom:* Four I think.

*Teacher:* Call that number 4, then for the chorus it goes up to number 4.

*Student:* Let's put the beat on and then do the song.

*Student:* Wait, wait. (Messing about).

*Student:* Put the beat on.

*Student:* Let's do the beat, do the guitars, you can sing.

*Student:* Play the song, play the song!

Here the teacher is:

- Asking the students whether they need any help, then drawing them in by showing interest and asking a student to demonstrate what he can do.

- Drawing in another student by asking if he remembered what he had done the previous week and to demonstrate it.

- Responding to students' requests for help with parts that they do not yet know.

- Working out chords and seeking a "missing note" by ear, thus demonstrating the trial-and-error process.

- Asking a student to listen and count the number of riffs he can hear before the chorus should start; then using that as a basis for the group to know where the chorus comes in.

The following comments express the perspectives of four highly experienced teachers concerning the strategies in the informal classroom, in particular what they themselves learnt from putting these approaches into action.

> So, for example, the kids doing Coldplay were trying to work out some notes, and instead of trying to leap in and work out the notes, I just stood there while this kid tried the notes and then he just found them. . . . And they will find the way themselves, and that came as a little bit of a surprise. I thought they would need a lot more input, a lot more guidance from me as a teacher, but I think they,

97

in a lot of respects, have found the answers themselves, from the things they've asked. . . . So within the space of two weeks, when I hadn't actually been able to put in any input and make any suggestions, they had done it themselves.

What I've been able to do is to go into groups, ask them questions, and then actually wait for them to come back with the answers themselves, rather than me having any particular in-put. . . . I was in a group last week, went in, "How did you get on today?" and they said "Oh it wasn't very good." So I was able just to say to them "What, why wasn't it very good?" And they told me exactly why, and then looked for the next question. So I said "What will you do about it?" And they came up with two almost, you know, perfect suggestions of things to try, and they've then tried it. And I think the effect that has on them is that they have found the way themselves, they know they've found the way themselves, and today they've done a performance which demonstrates how effective that's been, and that they can put together a piece of music from, from nothing. . . . So I was questioning them in a completely different way, I wasn't leading them in any respect, I was just giving them the opportunity to speak out. It's a completely different way of questioning from when *you've* got the answer in your head, you want them to say the word "dynamics" and you're going to get them to say the word "dynamics" for as long as it takes you to do it. It's different—it doesn't matter.

It's shown me that a lot of pressure and over-pacing of stuff isn't always a good idea. And I think leaving children to actually think and contemplate and listen and analyse, and then try stuff out and be able to do that without having a five-minute time limit, or a seven-and-a-half-minute time limit, or whatever time that you put on it, has certainly benefited a lot of children and there has been a sense of, sort of laid-backness with this, but which has still produced results which I've been impressed with really. . . . I think, you know, you can learn a lot from that as a classroom teacher. We're so into pace and everything's going zap, zap, zap, zap and flashing lights and cartwheels and all the rest of it. And I think, especially with a subject like music, we need to argue our corner really as music teachers, because children need time to contemplate, think, and consider, listen and try stuff out, and practise, and this is a word which is out of fashion in education, "practice." You need to practise stuff, and you need a lot of time to do that. And we don't give them time.

Photo © Emile Holba,
www.emileholba
.co.uk, courtesy of
Musical Futures,
www.musicalfutures
.org

# 20

# What were the overall views of the participants?

Classroom teachers have generally observed outstanding advances in students' enjoyment and motivation, and music has become a highly popular subject in many of the schools that are putting the approach into practice. Teachers often feel that being allowed to choose their own music and direct their own learning strategies are two significant aspects of students' motivation.

> It has been highly motivational. I really believe that . . . kids who wouldn't take that outside the classroom—if that makes sense—they have done with this. . . . It's linked into their lives, 'cause it's hit on their culture, their music culture, and what they like.

> They have certainly been highly motivated, for the vast, vast, vast majority of the time. Nobody's ever disliked it; I mean that's a significant thing; I think it's unanimous really. They've all very much enjoyed it for the reasons I think I've probably already outlined—the choice, working at their own pace, and they've been allowed to set the standards.

> The initial impact, the initial motivation, you know it's like they're setting, you know, a bomb alight! They just went for it. It was a massive sort of development in their ideas.

Students themselves also reported high levels of enthusiasm and enjoyment.

> We had only just started the year, everyone was still like mucking about and trying to make their friends again. And this really got everyone awake!

> I thought it was good, it was fun, it was a challenge, and I enjoyed it, I really enjoyed it.

> It's well fun—it's probably our best lesson so far.

> It's unlike any other lesson that we've done before.

> I'd prefer music if it was like this for like the whole of school.

Increased motivation was linked, by both teachers and students, to an increased application and willingness to settle down to the task, which in its turn was linked to the greater level of autonomy being invested in the students. Students also particularly valued being trusted to work on their own, being given a choice of what music to play (in stages 1 and 3), and being given a choice of which instruments to play.

*Teachers:* I think it really works in terms of the motivation of the students, of their enthusiasm, and it actually has had effects on the behaviour of students too. So I've seen really marked improvements in how many students stay on task, how you can actually leave students in a room, with instruments, and they will do the work that they are expected to do.

In terms of motivation, they come in, they're ready to work, and they know what they've got to do. They don't need the normal introductions to what they've got to do, they know where they're at. They've already decided what they've got to do when they walk out of one lesson, they've already thought about it by the time they come to the next lesson.

*Students:* We came up with our own ideas and it was fun. We weren't being told what to do, and the teachers put trust in us.

When you do what you want you enjoy it more, whereas if you get a set task and you don't like it then you're not exactly going to try your hardest are you?

If you teach yourself, you feel better, 'cause you realise that like you've done it all by yourself.

You learn more by trial and error—what works, what doesn't work. Like in previous years we've just been told "Right, this is what you've got to play, you've got to do it like this," whereas this one we've been able to choose what we play and how we play it.

You can learn more by yourself; you can experiment; there's no one telling you it's wrong; you can't do nothing wrong.

Another reason for the increased motivation is that the students are given more time in which to learn, with less pressure to demonstrate quick results. This was something that many teachers felt they had learnt about their own approaches to teaching:

*Teachers:* I've learnt that things don't just last a lesson. I'm very quick paced when I do things, and sometimes if I see one person off task I will stop it and bring everybody in 'cause I want everyone to be focused the whole time. And maybe I'm stopping people from developing further by not giving them that time.

It takes them a few weeks to actually build the confidence to attempt things, and I find that students need the consistency to feel confident in what they're doing. And if it takes a couple of weeks of being with the same instruments, with the same group, with the same CD to actually build that confidence, I think it's really important that we allow for it.

As teachers we're always working to a really tight timescale, and to lesson objectives, every lesson must be this structured thing, and I don't think we really give them the space to explore actually working as groups and doing those things. And then when it does come together, then they do get the motivation from actually having achieved something. But I didn't realise that before—I'm only starting to realise that now.

This approach allows the students time to absorb. I suppose that's it, isn't it? It's the absorption of music and letting it come out again.

It's about giving them space to create their group ethos before they start, and working in friendship groups and just being prepared to trust them.

The final statement above links into the perceived importance of allowing the students to choose their own friendship groups. This is important for many reasons. One is that, as both teachers and students themselves identified, students are more likely to enjoy the task and to cooperate if they are allowed to work with friends. But there are also reasons to do with musical taste. The task involves choosing and agreeing on a piece of music to play, and this relies on a certain level of shared taste. Particularly amongst teenagers, musical taste is one of the defining characteristics of their identity and, therefore, of how they choose their friends. This was particularly mentioned by students.

*Students:* I feel better if I get it wrong when I'm with my friends.

We got to like pick our groups at the start so we could work with people that we knew we could get on with.

No, we cooperated—because we're mates and so, it was easy.

It's better when you, it's better when you're with your friends really, 'cause like you get on with it a bit better. . . . 'Cause when you're not with your friends, like, and when you're with other people you don't really like, you're like always arguing and it wastes time of like rehearsing.

Last year when we were sitting in the classroom, there are people in your group who are like naughty and they always get told off. But this time because you're on your own, with your friends, you just get on with it and you do it how you want to.

One of the most important findings, that is already evident in the comments above, was that group organisation and cooperation were often enhanced. This was noted by both teachers and students. Many of them said that as well as musical skills, the students learnt group cooperation skills.

*Teachers:* There's been very little arguing, very little fighting, they've split if they want to split, they've carried on if they want to carry on—that's really impressive.

They worked brilliantly as groups. They cooperated, they were all contributing as well so their work had a sense of purpose, and they were all working towards creating a good performance.

*Students:* We listened to each other and then gave advices on how to improve, and that was like helpful for each other.

We've got used to each others' different style of playing—now we know everyone's ability we know what they can do.

I'm really pleased because of like what we can do and what we have done. It's all about teamwork.

We like helped each other and everything. We like took, every week we'd help each other on different instruments.

I think I've learnt to, like, work more as a team, like listen to each other, whereas before like I used to like always be speaking over everyone kind of thing, but I've like got used to working as a group now better.

Teachers often expressed surprise at how much ability and autonomy the students demonstrated:

They will find the way themselves, and that came as a little bit of a surprise. I thought they would need a lot more input, a lot more guidance from me as a teacher, yet they found the answers themselves.

The fact that there is no pressure on them, that they can just show what they've done, is a positive experience—as much as we can make it for them. I suppose that's what is so different about the project than normal class teaching.

Students who had previously been identified as disaffected were often mentioned as having completely changed their attitudes—again, both by teachers and by students themselves. Signs of musical ability, interest, and/or leadership qualities emerged, particularly in some students who had not previously shown such qualities.

*Teachers:*

I was completely gob-smacked to see Scott singing in front of the whole class. I wouldn't have got that. I mean, I've got boys in my choir, but, you know, they're not that kind of Year 9 kid who will just not have a care and just sing. We were really thrilled with that actually. I was really thrilled with the girls as well just singing.

I was really surprised to see Barjinda organising his group like that.

Luke is a disaffected kid. I'm going to show you his report from last year, I've got a copy for you. He got nothing but Ds and Es. This year he's got A all the way through—for effort and achievement.

*Students:*

I think my behaviour grade has gone up. Because like when you're in the classroom just doing like written and stuff, you get bored and you just muck around and stuff. But when you're doing this you can't get bored.

We were kind of silly at first and then we realised by ourselves that we had to get on with it.

The system of each individual working at his own level at the same task was noted. It was generally agreed that the task was accessible to those with low ability and little or no prior instrumental experience, yet stretched the high ability students and those who had instrumental skills:

*Teachers:*

Regardless of their ability this is something that everybody can succeed in at their own level because they're making their own choices about what they play, and with a bit of input from us to help them find a drum beat or a chord pattern it is possible for them all to access this at their own level.

I think they feel very equal actually, because it's not a case of "Oh, you're good at music" or whatever—they feel quite on a par with each other, so that's good.

*Students:*

I don't like being given something really easy to do, 'cause then it's just boring as you know what to do straight away.

We just like chose a part that would like fit our abilities, so like if we were good we would play something that was quite difficult, but if we weren't as good we'd just play something that was quite easy.

It's good in a way, like, so people can learn on their own what to do and to build up self-confidence.

You get to know a bit about the instrument that you're playing and it gives you a chance to work on your own and see how much you can achieve by yourself.

Some students also expressed a feeling of pride about what they had managed to achieve; and this seemed to be enhanced by the fact that rather than being directly "taught," they had "done it themselves."

Because it was really hard getting it all together, when we actually performed to the class we were all really proud of ourselves.

This gives you the chance to prove what you're capable of.

In relation to the development of musical skills, many teachers felt that basic ensemble, rhythmic, and instrumental skills developed:

They don't realise that they're actually playing really well in time together without a backing track to keep them, and they're actually developing really essential skills like that—ensemble skills, definitely, and also group work skills of listening to each other and having to put something together has really improved, dramatically.

Most particularly, teachers considered that students' listening skills developed significantly. Many students echoed this, often saying they were beginning to understand more about how music is put together and that their listening skills had developed. A number of them remarked that before the project they listened just to lyrics, and that only after having done the ear-playing exercise did they realise that music was made up in "layers."

*Teachers:*

They're learning to use their ears a lot more—aural skills, differentiating—a lot of students are able to do that. Listening to bass lines and picking out percussion parts. They are doing that more than I ever dreamed they would.

Their listening skills are so integrated in what they're doing, it is almost unique in that respect. Because normally listening skills are sat behind a desk where everybody listens at the same time, and in this they can listen as many times as they want with a focus on any particular aspect of the music that they want to do. And I think that that is as integrated as listening can be, really.

*Students:*

I've been listening to music recently and I've like kind of picked up the different rhythms and stuff. . . . I wouldn't have picked those up before, I don't think.

I listen to the instruments whilst playing in the background. Before I used to watch the musicians, see how they dance (*laughs*). Now as I listen to it—the instruments, how they're playing in the background—I try to figure out what instrument they use.

If I hear a song I'm like "Oh that's a well cool song," but when I actually think about it then I'd notice like all of the different things that had to go into it. We just think people just like bash the drums or whatever. But it's a lot harder than that, 'cause you have to like get the same beat all the way through, and you've got to try and remember some bits, and it gets difficult.

Yeah, 'cause I used to just hear the beat and the lyrics, but now I can hear more stuff that actually sounds really good in the song. 'Cause it used to be like just a block of music.

Like, usually in a song you listen to the words and the rhythms, but after this you started to learn the beats and the basic instruments they're using.

One feeling was that the students were engaged somehow with "real" music and "real" musical skills, the implication being that the classroom has a tendency to make tasks somehow "educational" rather than "real." Here, the aim is to join up the two.

*Teacher:* They can walk away thinking "I can play an instrument!" I've been quite staggered actually.

105

*Students:*

I've actually learnt more about music, my grade has gone up in music, my attitude has gone up in music, and I enjoy music more.

I've learnt more in this than I did in the whole of music last year.

You're becoming a musician, I suppose.

This way we can actually learn about *music*.

# Appendices

# APPENDIX A    Findings from an aural test experiment

As part of the work with instrumental teachers (part 1 of this handbook), we conducted a "matched pairs" experiment. The aim was to see if the HeLP strategies caused any improvements in aural abilities that were discernable at a level above and beyond the stated opinions of teachers and students, and the observations of researchers. The experiment involved materials of the kind used in formal grade exams (see Note on the text for an explanation of the British-based grade system). We were extremely grateful to the major examination body, the Associated Board of the Royal Schools of Music (ABRSM: <www.abrsm.org.uk>) who kindly supplied us with the materials for the tests as well as participating in the assessment exercise.

We asked four teachers to select matched pairs of students: two students who had been playing for roughly the same length of time, on the same instrument, at roughly the same standard, and were roughly the same age. Altogether there were thirty-two students involved: five flautists, three clarinetists, two alto saxophonists, and the rest were pianists, aged from ten to fourteen.

Each student listened to a short recording of a melody played twice on a piano. The student was then given the starting note and key chord, but nothing else, and was asked to play the melody back on their instrument, by ear. First all the participants were individually tested, and their performances were audio recorded. This formed the baseline test to discern the levels of the students before the intervention of the HeLP strategies. Then, one student from each matched pair was randomly allocated to group A, the "experimental group"—the group that went on to do the HeLP strategies; and the other one to group B, the "control group"—the group that did not use any HeLP strategies. All the students in group A then undertook the HeLP strategies for seven to ten lessons, one lesson per week, for a period of about ten to fifteen minutes per lesson. The students in group B carried on with their normal weekly lesson. At the end of the seven-to-ten-week period, all the students were tested and recorded again.

A panel of judges was formed, which included eighteen teachers from the project, two of the researchers, and two independent experts (the chief examiner and the syllabus director from the Associated Board of the Royal Schools of Music in the UK). On three separate occasions, members of the panel listened to the audio recordings of the children's performances in random order, without knowing whether they were listening to a baseline test or a postintervention test, or whether they were listening to a student from group A or group B. Thus no bias can have been involved in the assessments.

Each performance of each student was assessed using a five-point rating scale, with 1 = Very poor, 2 = Poor, 3 = Medium, 4 = Good, and 5 = Very good. A point was given for each of the six following criteria:

- Pitch accuracy
- Contour accuracy
- Rhythmic accuracy
- Closure

- Tempo accuracy
- Overall performance

Whereas most of these terms are already largely understood between educators and musicians, in some areas we gave a little explanation. The appraisers were told that the term "closure" referred to whether the candidate petered out halfway through and came to a standstill; or, having petered out, recovered and attempted the final two notes. A student who gave up in the middle might attract a Poor or Very Poor tick for that criterion; someone who stopped in the middle, then attempted the last two notes with some confidence, with or without the correct pitches, might achieve Medium; and someone who stopped in the middle but then played the final two notes correctly might achieve Good or Very good, for that criterion.

By "Tempo accuracy" as distinct from "Rhythmic accuracy" we referred to conditions where the student may, for example, accurately reproduce the whole rhythm but at a slower pace than the recorded excerpt. This would attract a "Good" tick for rhythm, but a "Poor" tick for tempo. Conversely, there were cases where students played the wrong rhythm but nonetheless with a regular pulse at the right tempo.

In addition to these criteria, "Level Descriptors" provided by the ABRSM were also included in the assessments. These were designed in consultation with the board and, as such, were a familiar, relevant format for the instrumental teachers concerned. They are shown in figure 9 below.

**Figure 9**
ABRSM level descriptors

| | |
|---|---|
| 17–18 | *Very good—Distinction* |
| | Fluent, accurate, and a prompt response |
| 15–16 | *Good—Merit* |
| | At tempo, with some inaccuracy, omission or hesitation. Musical details conveyed |
| 12–14 | *Medium—Pass* |
| | Outline in place, despite inaccuracy and hesitation |
| 9–11 | BELOW PASS STANDARD |
| | *Poor—Fail* |
| | Uncertain and an inaccurate response. Frequent errors |
| 6–8 | *Very poor—Fail* |
| | Very hesitant and a mostly incorrect or incomplete response |
| 0 | No work offered |

The findings were that all the children in the group who had used the HeLP strategies achieved higher marks on every criterion than did the students who had not used the HeLP strategies. Charts showing this are provided in figures 10–16. On the one hand, it should be remembered that these results were achieved after the children had been using the HeLP strategies for only seven to ten weeks and in that sense they are persuasive. On the other hand, these figures are complex to interpret fully, and some of them are not necessarily statistically significant in a technical sense. A full, technical analysis will be available in Baker and Green, "Ear Playing and Aural Development: Results from a 'Case-Control' Experiment" (2013).

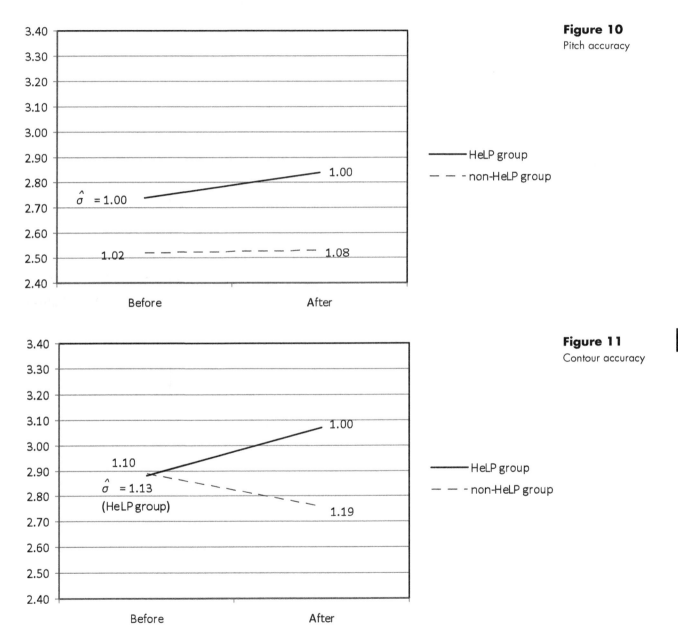

**Figure 10**
Pitch accuracy

**Figure 11**
Contour accuracy

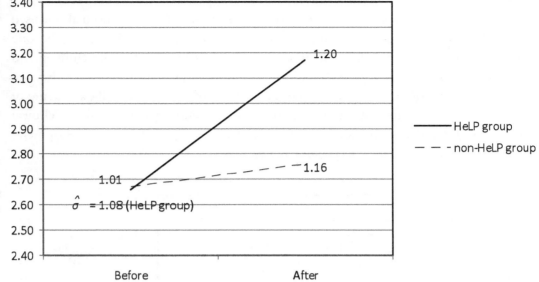

**Figure 12**
Rhythmic accuracy

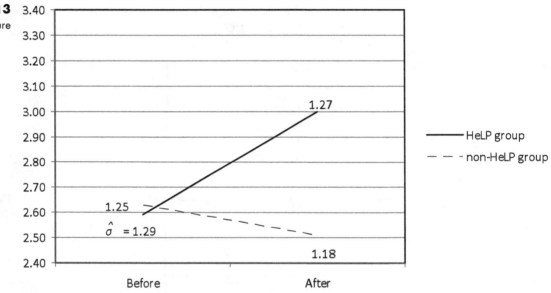

**Figure 13**
Closure

114

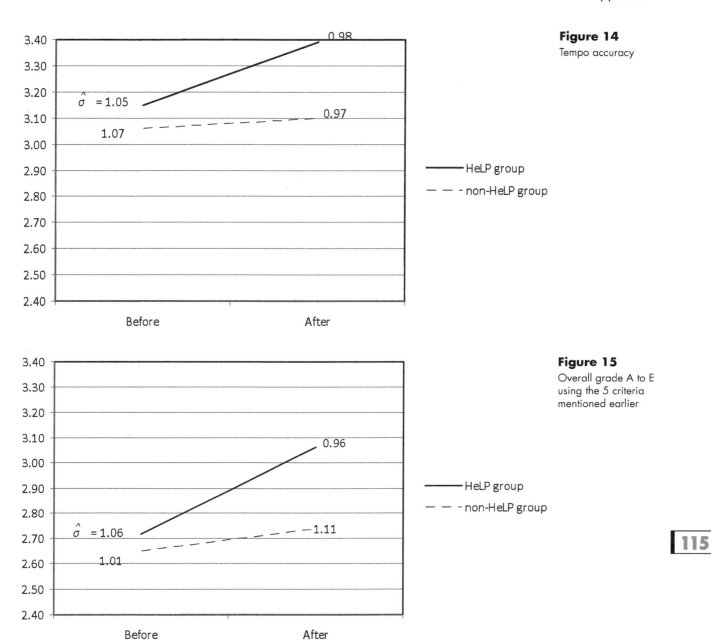

**Figure 14**
Tempo accuracy

**Figure 15**
Overall grade A to E
using the 5 criteria
mentioned earlier

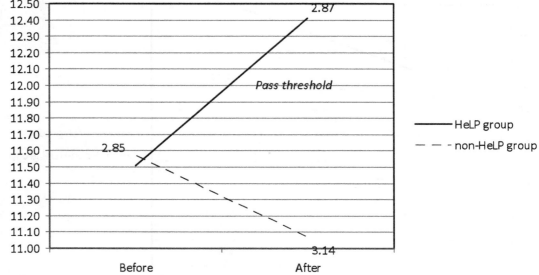

**Figure 16**
Overall grade using
the ABRSM criteria

# APPENDIX B    The research behind this handbook

## Books

Green, Lucy. 2001. *How Popular Musicians Learn: A Way Ahead for Music Education.* London: Ashgate Press.

————. 2008. *Music, Informal Learning and the School: A New Classroom Pedagogy.* London: Ashgate Press.

## Articles and book chapters

Baker, David. 2013. "Music, Informal Learning and the Instrumental Lesson: Teacher and Student Evaluations of the Ear Playing Project (EPP)." In *Developing the Musician,* edited by Mary Stakelum, 291–310. London: Ashgate Press

Baker, David, and Lucy Green. 2013. "Ear Playing and Aural Development: Results from a 'Case-Control' Experiment," Research Studies in Music Education, 35, no. 2.

Green, Lucy. 2004. "What Can Teachers Learn from Popular Musicians?" In *Bridging the Gap: Popular Music and Education,* edited by Carlos Rodriguez, 225–41. American Music Educators' National Conference: The National Association for Music Education.

————. 2005. "The Music Curriculum as Lived Experience: Children's 'Natural' Music Learning Processes." Special issue, *Music Educators' Journal* 19, no. 4: 27–32. Also available in *Music and Human Beings—Music and Identity,* edited by Börje Stålhammar, 15–27. Sweden: Universitetsbiblioteket.

————. 2006. "Popular Music Education in and for Itself, and for 'Other' Music: Current Research in the Classroom." Special issue, *International Journal of Music Education* 24, no. 2: 101–18.

————. 2008. "Group Co-operation, Inclusion and Disaffected Students: Some Responses to Informal Learning in the Music Classroom." *Music Education Research* 10, no. 2: 177–92.

————. 2012a. "Informal Learning and Aural Learning in the Instrumental Music Lesson: Findings from a Research-and-Development Pilot Project." In *Future Prospects for Music Education: Corroborating Informal Learning Pedagogy*, edited by Lauri Vakeva and Sidsel Karlsen. Cambridge: Cambridge Scholars Press.

————. 2012b. "Musical 'Learning Styles' and 'Learning Strategies' in the Instrumental Lesson: Some Emergent Findings from a Pilot Study." *Psychology of Music* 40, no. 1: 42–65.

Varvarigou, Maria, and Lucy Green. In preparation. "Musical Learning Styles and Strategies in the Instrumental Music Lesson: Main Study Findings."

## Other publications directly concerning Musical Futures

Below is a small selection of work which arises directly out of Musical Futures or is closely connected with it in some way. More such work is constantly being published.

Chua, Siew Ling. 2013. "Informal Learning for Song Writing." In *Connecting the Stars: Essays on Student-centric Music Education,* edited by S. L. Chua and H. P. Ho, 87–97. Singapore: Singapore Teachers' Academy for the Arts, Ministry of Education. http://www.star.moe.edu.sg/resources/star-research-repository

————. 2013. "STOMPing Up Musical Engagement the Non-formal and Informal Way." In Chua Ho, *Connecting the Stars*, 127–42.

Chua, Siew Ling, and Hui Ping Ho. 2013. "Piloting Informal and Non-formal Approaches for Music Teaching in Five Secondary Schools in Singapore: *An Introduction.*" In Chua and Ho, *Connecting the Stars,* 52–65.

————. 2013. "Connecting Findings, Reflections and Insights: Student-centricity Musically, Creatively." In Chua and Ho, *Connecting the Stars,* 143–54.

Costes-Onish, Pamela. 2013. "Negotitating the Boundaries of Formal and Informal Learning." In Chua and Ho. *Connecting the Stars,* 98–109.

D'Amore, Abigail, ed. 2011. Musical Futures: *An Approach to Teaching and Learning: Resource Pack*, 2nd ed. London: Paul Hamlyn Foundation. www.musicalfutures.org.

Gower, Anna. 2012. "Integrating Informal Learning Approaches into the Formal Learning Environment of Mainstream Secondary Schools in England." *British Journal of Music Education* 29, no. 1: 13–18.

Hallam, Susan, Andrea Creech, Clare Sandford, Tiija Rinta, and Katherine Shave. 2008. *Survey of Musical Futures: A Report from Institute of Education University of London.* London: Paul Hamlyn Foundation, www.musicalfutures.org.

Ho, Hui Ping. 2013. "Rollin' in at the Deep End: *Choice, Collaboration and Confidence through Informal Learning with the Guitar.*" In Chua and Ho, *Connecting the Stars,* 66–85.

————. 2013. "Connecting the Curricular and Co-curricular through Formal and Non-formal Teaching." In Chua and Ho, *Connecting the Stars,* 110–26).

Jeanneret, Neryl, Rebecca McLennan, and Jennifer Stevens-Ballenger. 2011. *Musical Futures: An Australian Perspective: Findings from a Victorian Pilot Study.* Melbourne: University of Melbourne. www.musicalfuturesaustralia.org.

O'Neill, Susan, and Kevin Bespflug. 2012. "Musical Futures Comes to Canada: Engaging Students in Real-world Music Learning.' *Canadian Music Educator* 53, no. 2: 25–34.

Price, David. 2005. *Musical Futures: An Emerging Vision.* London: Paul Hamlyn Foundation. www.musicalfutures.org.

————. 2006. *Personalising Music Learning.* London: Paul Hamlyn Foundation. www.musicalfutures.org.

Wright, Ruth. 2011. "Musical Futures: A New Approach to Music Education." *Canadian Music Educator* 53, no. 2: 19–21.

————. 2012. "Tuning into the Future: Sharing Initial Insights about the 2012 Musical Futures Pilot Project in Ontario." *Canadian Music Educator* 53, no. 4: 14–18.

# APPENDIX C   Related work on informal music learning in music education

Appendix C gives a small selection of other publications examining some ways in which informal music learning practices can relate to formal music education contexts. There is now so much work in this area, and so much more constantly being added, that the list makes no pretence to being complete, and my apologies to those who might feel their work has been overlooked. There is also a significant and growing bibliography on informal learning in many other musical styles, which has not been included here.

Abrahams, Frank, Dan Abrahams, Anthony Rafaniello, Jason Vodicka, David Westawski, and John Wilson. 2011. "Going Green: The Application of Informal Music Learning Strategies in High School Choral and Instrumental Ensembles," http://www.rider.edu/wcc/academics/center-critical-pedagogy/our-research.

Andrews, Kathryn. 2013. "Standing 'On Our Own Two Feet': A Comparison of Teacher-Directed and Group Learning in an Extra-curricular Instrumental Group." *British Journal of Music Education*, 30, no. 1:125–48.

Byrne, C., and M. Sheridan. 2000. "The Long and Winding Road: The Story of Rock Music in Scottish Schools." *International Journal of Music Education* 36:46–58.

Campbell, Patricia Shehan. 1995. "Of Garage Bands and Song-Getting: The Musical Development of Young Rock Musicians." *Research Studies in Music Education* 4 ( June): n.p.n.

———. 1998. *Songs in Their Heads: Music and its Meaning in Children's Lives.* New York: Oxford University Press.

Cayari, Christopher. 2013. "Using Informal Education Through Music Video Creation." *General Music Today*, published online 11 July 2013. http://gmt.sagepub.com/content/early/2013/07/10/1048371313492537.

Davis, S. G. 2005. "'That Thing You Do!' Compositional Processes of a Rock Band." *International Journal of Education and the Arts* 6, no. 16: 189–200.

Downey, Jean. 2009. "Informal Learning in Music in the Irish Secondary School Context." *Action, Criticism and Theory in Music Education* 8, no. 2: 47–60.

Evelein, F. 2006. "Pop and World Music in Dutch Music Education: Two Cases of Authentic Learning in Music Teacher Education and Secondary Music Education." *International Journal of Music Education* 24, no. 2: 178–87.

Feichas, Heloisa. 2010. "Informal Music Learning Practices as a Pedagogy of Integration in Brazilian Higher Education." *British Journal of Music Education* 27, no. 1: 47–58.

Finney, John, and Christopher Philpott. 2010. "Student Teachers Appropriating Informal Pedagogy." *British Journal of Music Education* 27, no. 1: 7–19.

Finnegan, R. 1989. *The Hidden Musicians: Music-Making in an English Town.* Cambridge: Cambridge University Press.

Folkestad, G. 2006. "Formal and Informal Learning Situations or Practices versus Formal and Informal Ways of Hearing." *British Journal of Music Education* 23, no. 2: 135–45.

Gatien, Greg. 2009. "Categories and Music Transmission." *Action, Criticism and Theory in Music Education* 8, no. 2: 95–120.

Georgii-Hemming, E., and M. Westvall. 2010. "Examining Current Discourses of Music Education in Sweden." *British Journal of Music Education* 27, no. 1: 21–33.

Jaffurs, S. E. 2004. "The Impact of Informal Music Learning Practices in the Classroom, or How I Learned How to Teach from a Garage Band." *International Journal of Music Education* 22, no. 3: 189–200.

Karlsen, Sidsel. 2010. "BoomTown Music Education/Authenticity: Informal Music Learning in Swedish Post-Compulsory Music Education." *British Journal of Music Education* 27, no. 1: 35–46.

Lebler, Don. 2007. "Student as Master? Reflections on a Learning Innovation in Popular Music Pedagogy." *International Journal of Music Education* 25, no. 30: 205–21.

———. 2008. "Popular Music Pedagogy: Peer Learning in Practice." *Music Education Research* 10, no. 2: 193–213.

Lines, David. 2009. "Exploring the Contexts of Informal Learning." *Action, Criticism and Theory in Music Education* 8, no. 2: 1–7.

Mans, Minette. 2009. "Informal Learning and Values." *Action, Criticism and Theory in Music Education* 8, no. 2: 80–94.

Marsh, Kathryn. 1999. "Mediated Orality: The Role of Popular Music in the Changing Traditions of Children's Musical Play." *Research Studies in Music Education* 13, no. 1: 2–12.

———. 2008. *The Musical Playground: Global Tradition and Change in Children's Songs and Games.* Oxford: Oxford University Press

McPhail, Graham. 2012. "Knowledge and the Curriculum: Music as a Case Study in Educational Futures." *New Zealand Journal of Educational Studies* 47, no. 1: 33–45.

———. 2013. "Developing Student Autonomy in the One-to-One Music Lesson." *International Journal of Music Education*, 31, no. 2: 160–72.

Nielsen, K. 2006. "Apprenticeship at the Academy of Music." *International Journal of Music Education* 7, no. 4: 1–15.

O'Flynn, John. 2006) "Vernacular Music-making and Education." *International Journal of Music Education* 24, no. 2: 140–47.

Rodriguez, Carlos, ed. 2004. *Bridging the Gap: Popular Music and Education.* American Music Educators' National Conference: The National Association for Music Education

———. 2009. "Informal Learning in Music: Emerging Roles of Teachers and Students." *Action, Criticism and Theory in Music Education* 8, no. 2: 36–47.

Siefried, S. 2006. "Exploring the Outcomes of Rock and Popular Music Instruction in High School Guitar Class: A Case Study." *International Journal of Music Education* 24, no. 2: 168–77.

Vakeva, Lauri. 2006. "Teaching Popular Music in Finland: What's up, What's ahead?" *International Journal of Music Education* 24, no. 2: 126–31.

———. 2009. "The World Well Lost, Found: Reality and Authenticity in Green's 'New Classroom Pedagogy.'" *Action, Criticism and Theory in Music Education* 8, no. 2: 8–35.

———. 2010. "Garageband or GarageBand? Remixing Musical Futures." *British Journal of Music Education* 27, no. 1: 59–70.

Vitale, John, L. 2011. "Formal and Informal Music Learning: Attitudes and Perspectives of Secondary School Non-Music Majors." *Teachers International Journal of Humanities and Social Science* 1, no. 5: 1–14.

Westerlund, H. 2006. "Garage Rock Bands: A Future Model for Developing Musical Expertise?" *International Journal of Music Education* 24, no. 2: 119–25.

Woody, R. H., and A. C. Lehmann. 2010. "Student Musicians' Ear-Playing Ability as a Function of Vernacular Music Experiences." *Journal of Research in Music Education* 58, no. 2: 101–15.

Wright, Ruth, and Panagiotis Kanellopoulos. 2010. "Informal Music Learning, Improvisation and Teacher Education. *British Journal of Music Education* 27, no. 1: 71–87.

# APPENDIX D    Websites

Three Musical Futures websites are in existence at the time of going to press:

http://www.musicalfutures.org (homepage)
http://musicalfuturescanada.org (homepage)
http://www.musicalfuturesaustralia.org (homepage)

The part of the UK Musical Futures site that relates primarily to the informal learning pathway is:

https://www.musicalfutures.org/resources/c/informallearning (informal learning page)

There is a smaller website on the Ear Playing Project's instrumental research:

http://earplaying.ioe.ac.uk

An interview with the author talking about the background to the research in both projects is available on:

http://www.youtube.com/watch?v=4r8zoHT4ExY

# APPENDIX E   Audio track list

**01 Dreaming, full (for any instruments)**

02 Dreaming (C), bass guitar

03 Dreaming (C), piano bass

04 Dreaming (C), piano 1

05 Dreaming (C), piano 2

06 Dreaming (C), piano 3

07 Dreaming (C), piano ad lib 1

08 Dreaming (C), piano ad lib 2

09 Dreaming (C), vibraphone 1

10 Dreaming (C), vibraphone 2

**11 Dreaming, full (for B-flat instruments, if desired)**

12 Dreaming (B-flat), bass guitar

13 Dreaming (B-flat), piano bass

14 Dreaming (B-flat), piano 1

15 Dreaming (B-flat), piano 2

16 Dreaming (B-flat), piano 3

17 Dreaming, (B-flat), piano ad lib 1

18 Dreaming (B-flat), piano ad lib 2

19 Dreaming (B-flat), vibraphone 1

20 Dreaming (B-flat), vibraphone 2

**21 Link Up, full**

22 Link Up, bass

23 Link Up, chords top

24 Link Up, chords middle

25 Link Up, chords bottom

26 Link Up, twiddle

27 Link Up, melody

**28 Mozart, *Eine Kleine Nachtmusik*, full**

29 Mozart, two parts

30 Mozart, melody A

31 Mozart, melody B

32 Mozart, bass A

33 Mozart, bass B

**34 Beethoven, "Für Elise," full**

35 Beethoven, two parts

36 Beethoven, melody A

37 Beethoven, melody B

38 Beethoven, bass A

39 Beethoven, bass B

**40 Clara Schumann, String Trio, full**

41 Clara Schumann, two parts

42 Clara Schumann, melody

43 Clara Schumann, bass

**44 Handel, Flute Sonata 5, minuet, full**

45 Handel, two parts

46 Handel, melody A

47 Handel, melody B

48 Handel, melody C

49 Handel, bass A

50 Handel, bass B

51 Handel, bass C

**52 Brahms, Symphony no. 1, mvt. 4 theme, full (arranged)**

53 Brahms, two parts

54 Brahms, melody A

55 Brahms, melody B

56 Brahms, bass A

57 Brahms, bass B

**58 Bach (Anna Magdalena) Minuet 3, full**

59 Bach, melody

60 Bach, bass

## APPENDIX F    Recording credits

### Tracks 1–20

Composed and arranged by Lucy Green
Sound engineering and production by Tim Smart

### Tracks 21–27

Performed and recorded by Daniel Spiller and the Broken Record Project
Daniel Spiller, guitar, vocals
Dani Mourinho, bass guitar
Mauro Pes, keyboard
Hezron Chetty, violin
Gareth Dylan Smith, drums, percussion
Composed and arranged by Lucy Green
Sound engineering by Daniel Spiller
Produced by Gareth Dylan Smith

### Tracks 28–60

Detta Danford, flute
Harriet Wheeler, violin
Josephine Wheeler, violin
Jennifer Edwards, viola
Max Roisi, cello
Lucy Green, piano/harpsichord/synthesizer
Arrangements by Lucy Green
Sound engineering by Evangelos Himonides